The Dark Side of Events

Navigating Corruption and Risk Management

William O'Toole

(G) Goodfellow Publishers Ltd

(G) Published by Goodfellow Publishers Limited,
26 Home Close, Wolvercote, Oxford OX2 8PS
http://www.goodfellowpublishers.com

British Library Cataloguing in Publication Data: a catalogue record for this title is available from the British Library.

Library of Congress Catalog Card Number: on file.

ISBN: 978-1-91509-799-6

DOI: 10.23912/9781915097415-5838

The Events Management Theory and Methods Series

Design and typesetting by P.K. McBride, www.macbride.org.uk

Series cover design by Cylinder

Geryon illustrations by Scarlet

Contents

The Stories

Introduction to the Events Management Theory and Methods Series

Event management as a field of study and professional practice has its textbooks with plenty of models and advice, a body of knowledge (EMBOK), competency standards (MBECS) and professional associations with their codes of conduct. But to what extent is it truly an applied management field? In other words, where is the management theory in event management, how is it being used, and what are the practical applications?

Event tourism is a related field, one that is defined by the roles events play in tourism and economic development. The primary consideration has always been economic, although increasingly events and managed event portfolios meet more diverse goals for cities and countries. While the economic aspects have been well developed, especially economic impact assessment and forecasting, the application of management theory to event tourism has not received adequate attention.

In this book series we launch a process of examining the extent to which mainstream theory is being employed to develop event-specific theory, and to influence the practice of event management and event tourism. This is a very big task, as there are numerous possible theories, models and concepts, and virtually unlimited advice available on the management of firms, small and family businesses, government agencies and not-for-profits. Inevitably, we will have to be selective.

The starting point is theory. Scientific theory must both explain a phenomenon, and be able to predict what will happen. Experiments are the dominant form of classical theory development. But for management, predictive capabilities are usually lacking; it might be wiser to speak of theory in development, or theory fragments. It is often the process of theory development that marks research in management, including the testing of hypotheses and the formulation of propositions. Models, frameworks, concepts and sets of propositions are all part of this development.

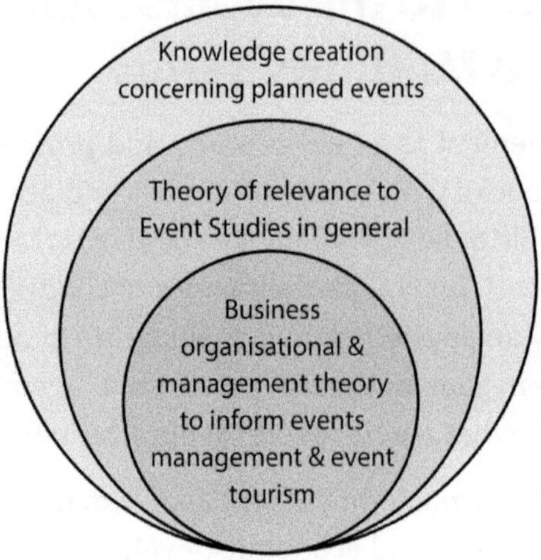

The diagram illustrates this approach. All knowledge creation has potential application to management, as does theory from any discipline or field. The critical factor for this series is how the theory and related methods can be applied. In the core of this diagram are management and business theories which are the most directly pertinent, and they are often derived from foundation disciplines.

All the books in this series will be relatively short, and similarly structured. They are designed to be used by teachers who need theoretical foundations and case studies for their classes, by students in need of reference works, by professionals wanting increased understanding alongside practical methods, and by agencies or associations that want their members and stakeholders to have access to a library of valuable resources. The nature of the series is that as it grows, components can be assembled by request. That is, users can order a book or collection of chapters to exactly suit their needs.

All the books will introduce the theory, show how it is being used in the events sector through a literature review, incorporate examples and case studies written by researchers and/or practitioners, and contain methods that can be used effectively in the real world.

A note from the author

This book was an inspiration after reading the Indian report on the Commonwealth Games. How did the well known, highly experienced companies get involved in this event quagmire? I knew some of the people involved and mentioned in the report. It is clearly written and makes no apologies. It can be seen as a manual of what not to do. This honesty is to be praised. Almost every form of corruption is found. The next inspiration was the Rio Olympics, I knew quite a few people from that region and they were disgusted at the corruption. Then I asked a few of them if they had ever slipped some money to a traffic cop. "Of course" was their reply. I walked away thinking that this huge corruption has been facilitated by petty street corruption. If people are used to small time facilitation payments, then a large scale bribe is just a matter of opportunity.

You will note that many of the standards used in this book are recent such as ISO 37002:2021, AS 8001-2021. It seems that it all developed quickly over the last years. At first there are specific country laws such as UK Bribery Act 2010, then the international convention that had been signed is enacted, then standards are created and the various companies and government department and local authorities adapt these standards to their circumstances.

When I started this research the anti-corruption and fraud policies were few and far between. Suddenly, in the space of less than a year, the web search went from a few hits to multiple pages. This uptake is remarkable.

The next step, I predict, is for all those entities to expect the companies they deal with to be aware of the standards, the issue of corruption and have an anti-corruption policy. It is mapped out in Figure 1. This includes event teams, event companies, boards, public festivals, conferences, venues, suppliers and more. All these can consult this book. Of course the information must be adapted to the special circumstances of the particular event. But the information and the references are there.

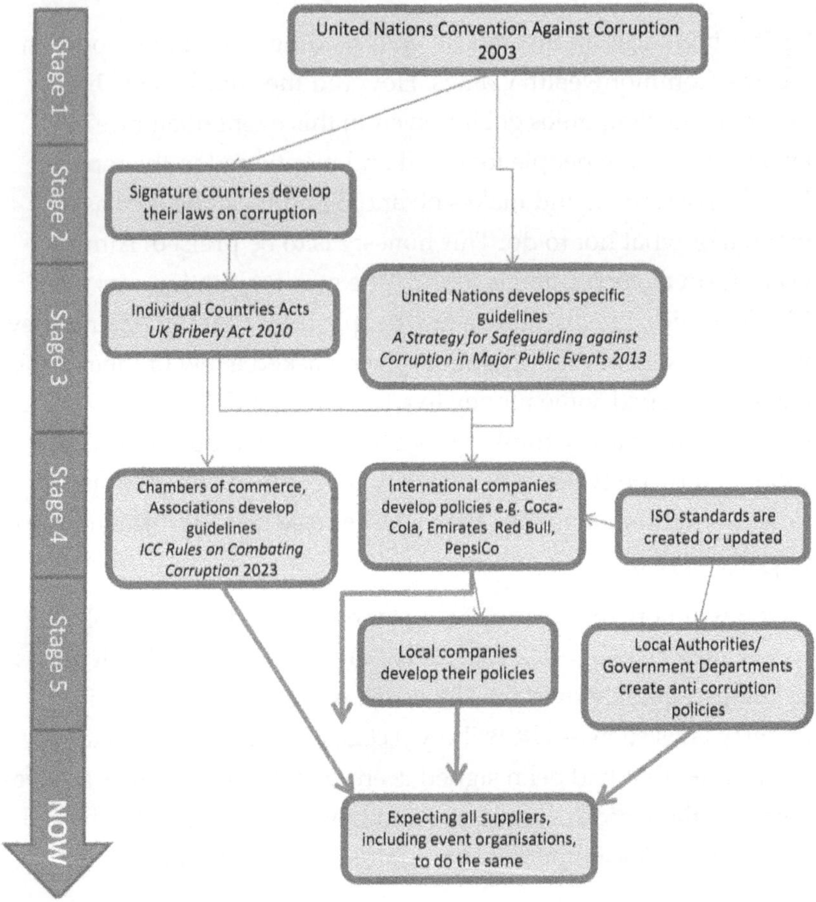

Figure 1: The timeline of combatting corruption requirements

Perhaps the most interesting aspect of writing this textbook manual was the lack of information coming in from event and festival organisers around the world. I asked, many times and received very little. But I knew from working in the events sector in over 50 countries, this was a real, ever present and ubiquitous issue. Some asked me why I was writing this, why bother? In my experience, this type of reluctance indicated the need for the book.

I knew in a few years they will be searching for information. It won't be long before proof of combatting corruption will be a requirement to bid for events or to work with sponsors and local governments. What I have written is to help them through this new confusion. As can be seen by the reference list, there is copious information and, to wade through it all will not help put on that event. With the stories, I have tried to make it as engaging as possible. It is actually not hard once the basis is understood. Really, it is plain ethics. Hence the many quotes from religions.

Over the years I have written about the events industry. It followed a path. From hands-on creating and managing a lot of special events, festivals, concerts around the world, I wrote about staging, logistics, the site and risk. Next step was a textbook on adapting project management to events. Using the project management model, I suggested the idea of the Event Management Body of Knowledge (EMBOK). From that it was a textbook on developing events and event strategies. Then back to risk management and crowds.

My conclusion from this experience was that the event sector over time could be described by a Maturity Model. It has followed many other professions and industry sectors. In one country, where I worked, it went from almost no public events to 12 public festivals around the country, each one worth hundreds of millions of USD.

At all times I was working developing events and event competency around the world, crossing borders, working in all kinds of cultures, cities and countries. It was a delight as I worked with the local people, creative people of high integrity, who want to make a difference, to help people celebrate life.

It is for them that I write about preventing corruption. As I write in the book, to corrupt means to take something good and make it bad. The event sector is a victim of its own success. It is a target. From the corrupt politicians to the petty criminal, they realise there is opportunity in events. They are moving in and we should be prepared. This textbook/manual is then the next stage in the event sector Maturity Model. It is absolutely necessary for the modern event world.

Thank you to Gracie Geikie of placeborneo.com, Katie, Steve Schmader, Di Henry, the ICAC and to the current and aspiring events people who attended my workshops in Uganda, Scotland, Sudan, Switzerland, Liberia, Abu Dhabi, Dubai, Canada, Qatar, KL, Aqaba, Bahrain, South Africa, Singapore, France, Kenya and most of the cities in USA, Australia, Saudi Arabia and New Zealand. Your expertise, integrity and passion have inspired me to write this book.

About the Author

William O'Toole is a global expert in event management. He began his career organizing concerts and tours in countries such as India, China, Russia, Nepal, Pakistan, and the USA. Concurrently, he founded an agency that pitched event concepts and managed events for both corporate clients and governments, including festivals, special events, product launches, and staff incentives. Drawing from this extensive experience, William authored the first international textbook on festival and event management, introducing the crucial topic of risk.

When the first risk standard was released, William proposed to the government that he train event teams in risk and project management. This standard was the basis of the ISO 31000, a standard now used worldwide. William has since worked as an events development consultant and trainer in over 30 countries, including Saudi Arabia, Jordan, Scotland, Liberia, the UAE, and South Africa. He also initiated the Event Management Body of Knowledge and was honoured as the 2018 inductee to the Hall of Fame by the International Festivals & Events Association for his significant contributions to the global development of festivals and events.

William has written and co-authored five international textbooks on event management, which have been translated into six languages. Currently, he teaches at the Master's level in France, Switzerland, and the USA.

"Ecco la fiera con la coda aguzza,che passa i monti e rompe i muri e l'armi! Ecco colei che tutto 'l mondo appuzza!".

"He's the beast whose poison none escapes. He breathes and soon the whole world falls into fever"

Clive James' rendering of Canto 17 first lines. Dante describes the Geryon or fraud, with the face of an honest man and the tail of a scorpion.

The beast, Geryon, is their guide to the last circle of Hell, Malebolge, the ditch of fraud, before they reach Inferno.

1 Introduction

The generally accepted definition of corruption is the abuse of entrusted power for private gain.

A more detailed definition is found in the AS 8001-2021: Fraud and Corruption Control, definition 1.4.8

> *" dishonest activity in which a person associated with an organisation (e.g. director, executive, manager, employee or contractor) acts contrary to the interests of the organisation and abuses their position of trust in order to achieve personal advantage or advantage for another person or organisation. This can also involve corrupt conduct by the organisation, or a person purporting to act on behalf of and in the interests of the organisation, in order to secure some form of improper advantage for the organisation either directly or indirectly."*
>
> Australian Standards. (2001)

The term 'private gain' can be misleading as people can act corruptly in order to further ideological aims. They may see their act as wrong, but necessary. They are concerned with the 'big picture' and justify their action as a pathway, i.e. the ends justify the means. In a sense there is a mathematics of consequence. The terrorist does not care about the ins and outs of bribery, their view is the larger moral picture.

As well, our concept of corruption is based on the pervading culture and norms. It may not translate well into other cultures. There is a subtlety to meaning. Although the group of people may nod in agreement when the topic of bribery, for example, is raised, what this means to each person could be very different. Professor Graycar uses the term 'protean'. Just like the Greek myth of Proteus, corruption can take very different forms and can look quite different to each person staring at it. (Graycar, 2015).

Bloom and others point out that the cultural aspect of corruption is too often ignored "*in a world of nearly global capitalism in favour of international laws and conventions*" (Bloom, 2013, p. 170). The concept of grease the wheels implies that some form of corruption is economically beneficial if the bureaucratic inertia in a country is an impediment to development (Méon & Weill, 2008). These larger issues are not discussed here. This book is concerned with on the ground, pragmatic, agreed upon meaning found in all the quotes that begin each of the sections.

Corruption is a worldwide problem. It can enter every area of government and business life. Any event team trying to find out how to prevent it is met with a myriad of documents and websites. It is only the big corruption, the ones to hit the press, which are noticed. It is almost impossible, and certainly impractical, to apply the lessons learned from the multi-million dollar mega corruption cases to the rest of the event sector. Certainly the mega events have been studied, and organisations such as the United Nations have excellent publications for mega events. These events have major infrastructure developed, stadiums built, often involve the various security arms of the government, multi-government and private contracts, high political involvement and consequences. Their close ties with governments mean they are subject to detailed public sector procurement policies, recruitment vetting policies and screening mechanisms.

But the average event does not have the time or resources to trawl through these cases, sort out what is relevant, what can be applied, then identify the vulnerabilities and forecast the consequences, intended or otherwise. Hence this textbook and manual.

The massive information has been scaled down to be applicable to events such as public celebrations, festivals, concerts, conferences, exhibitions and the like. Around the world there are millions of these. And they are all prone to corruption.

The aim is to prevent corruption. Like an infection, it can spread quickly, diminish the vitality of host and eventually lead to expiration. But far more than the host, it can easily spread to any company or person that has contact with the host. This virus is everywhere and waiting. It is impossible to destroy it completely, we can manage it. The tool recommended in this book is **risk management**.

As pointed out by Transparency International, corruption isn't limited to the misuse of power by government officials. For instance, it occurs when community leaders exploit their entrusted authority to represent community interests in dealings with the government and companies. People can engage in corrupt practices by misusing the power entrusted to them to act responsibly. This broader definition of corruption includes actions that may not be explicitly illegal. However, when individuals exploit their position, power, or privilege—whether legally or illegally—for personal gain or to benefit a select group, it still leads to detrimental effects on people, the environment, democratic institutions, and the economy, especially during negotiations with communities or the government. They add:

> *"Note that even if your country does not prohibit activities commonly considered corrupt, an individual or company engaging in certain corrupt activities may be liable to prosecution under the UK Bribery Act 2010 or the US Foreign Corrupt Practices Act 1977".*
> (Nest, 2020, p. 8).

An example of an act that is clearly unethical, but not necessarily illegal is an event company bidding for an event with no intention of running the event, but to drive up the price for competitors or to prevent them from bidding.

Just what is corruption. We all assume we know. We've seen it enough times in the movies, slipping the traffic cop a fiver to look the other way. But do have a think about it. When trying to find a definition is seems to be spinning in circles. Is it a crime? If there are no laws being broken is it still corruption? Does there have to be intent? Is it an ethical principle? Chapter 3 will discuss these issues as they include law and ethics. For the sake of our book, I will use the working definition above.

The follow chapters have three purposes.

A manual for organisations

It should be a manual for governments both local and state and for event teams and event companies around the world to evaluate their exposure to corruption. For this purpose there is a vulnerability assessment table. From the results, the event stakeholders should be able to establish an anti-corruption policy or guideline for the event that can fit with the policies of the sponsors and government departments. For this reason the textbook is written for use, not just study. The aim is to assist governments and events to diminish the risk of corruption.

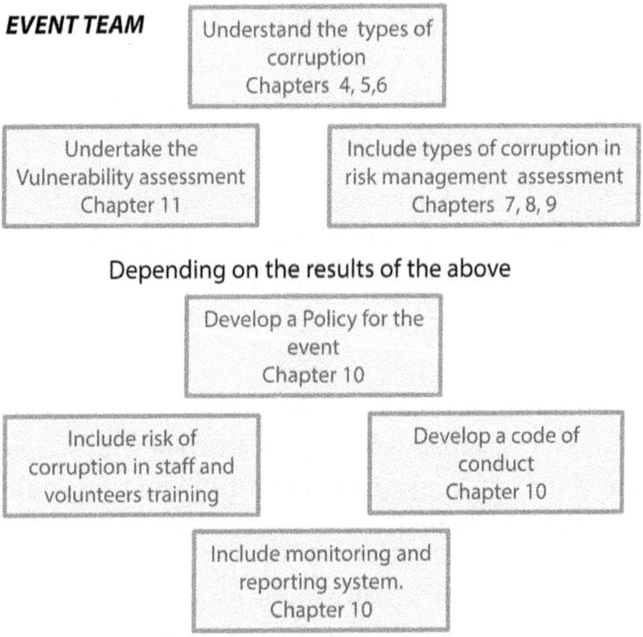
EVENT TEAM
Understand the types of corruption Chapters 4, 5,6
Undertake the Vulnerability assessment Chapter 11
Include types of corruption in risk management assessment Chapters 7, 8, 9
Depending on the results of the above
Develop a Policy for the event Chapter 10
Include risk of corruption in staff and volunteers training
Develop a code of conduct Chapter 10
Include monitoring and reporting system. Chapter 10

Figure 1.1: Event management team

There are very detailed and expansive books on the subject of corruption but most of the information is for large international companies and mega event. This is for the major, medium and minor events and for the governments that have to deal with them. Figure 1.1 illustrates how the information can be used for the team.

A textbook

Next it should be a textbook suitable for teaching this aspect of risk management at a tertiary level. For this to work there are separate chapters that can be turned into teaching topics. To assist this the theory is described as a framework subdivide into types of corruption and risk processes and tools. Each of these is illustrated with real stories and case studies. At the end of each chapter is a point by point summary that can be transferred to PowerPoint for the purpose of teaching and training. As well there are thought provoking questions and exercises to enable discussion. The exercises may be described as reflexive. The students must take part in discussions about real events and have an output to demonstrate the application of theory to an actual event to the other students. Figure 1.2 shows how the information in the book can be used for teaching.

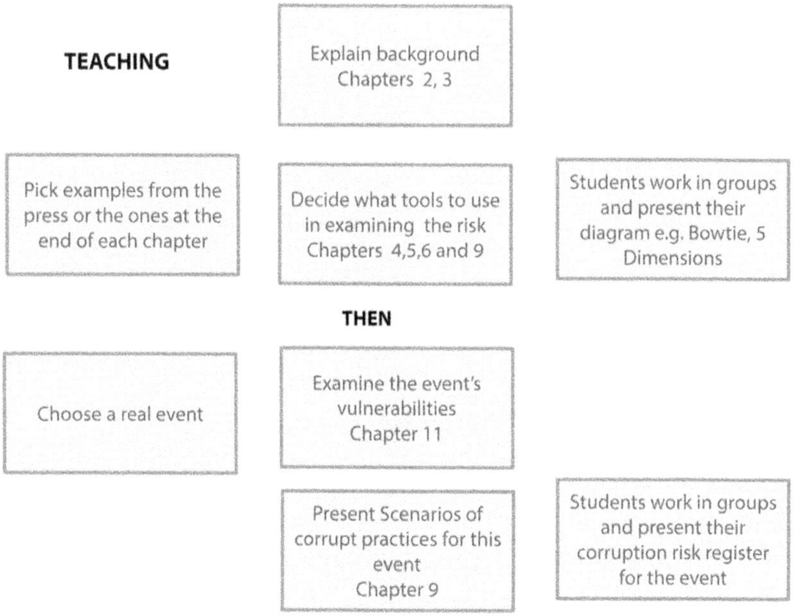
TEACHING
Explain background Chapters 2, 3
Pick examples from the press or the ones at the end of each chapter
Decide what tools to use in examining the risk Chapters 4,5,6 and 9
Students work in groups and present their diagram e.g. Bowtie, 5 Dimensions
THEN
Choose a real event
Examine the event's vulnerabilities Chapter 11
Present Scenarios of corrupt practices for this event Chapter 9
Students work in groups and present their corruption risk register for the event

Figure 1.2: Teaching students

Finally this book can be used for training event teams and those public officials responsible for events. The theme of the workshop should be "How to prevent and recognise corruption in event planning and execution". This will be achieved using a systematic methodology. Figure 1.3 illustrates how the information can be used in a training session for staff and volunteers.

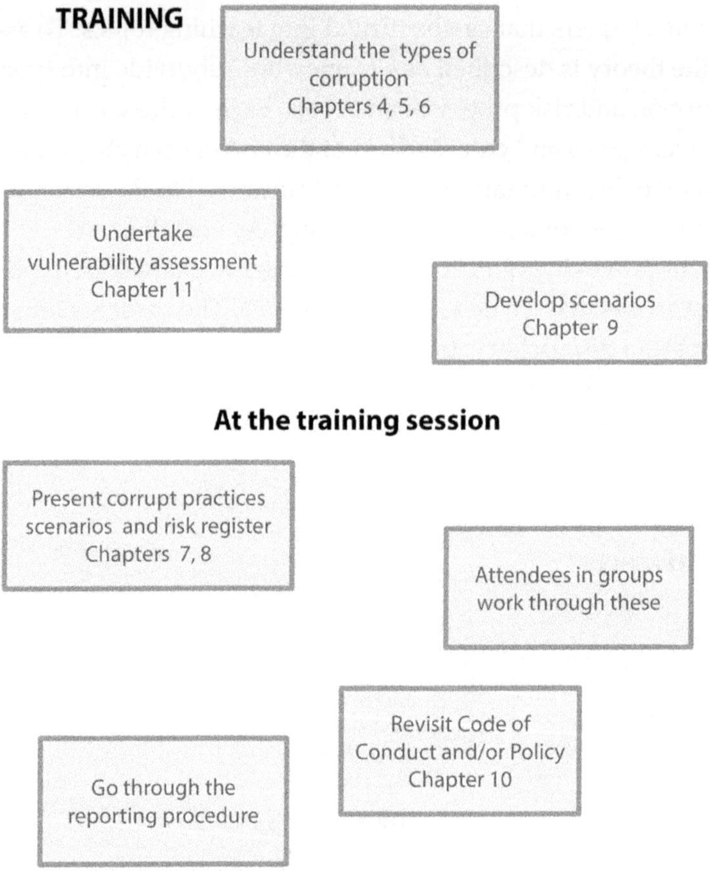
TRAINING
Understand the types of corruption
Chapters 4, 5, 6
Undertake vulnerability assessment
Chapter 11
Develop scenarios
Chapter 9
At the training session
Present corrupt practices scenarios and risk register
Chapters 7, 8
Attendees in groups work through these
Revisit Code of Conduct and/or Policy
Chapter 10
Go through the reporting procedure

Figure 1.3: Training staff and volunteers

There are already guidelines on mega events and sports events, but this book looks at corruption at the hundreds of thousands, if not millions, of major, medium and minor events. The local festival, the concert, community event, medical conference, beauty pageant. It is here where corruption starts and becomes acceptable.

Escalation is an important aspect of the broken windows theory in criminology. Minor infractions, if left unaddressed, can escalate into more serious criminal activities. The theory suggests that small signs of disorder signal that no one cares, leading to a breakdown of community controls. The small favours, bribes, fraud and other petty corruption create the acceptance and conditions for the corruption on a large scale. As pointed out in some of the academic studies, corruption as a mathematical model is similar to a virus. It spreads. Hence it must be at the event level and at the local authority level that corruption is prevented. It is here that the small bribe becomes leverage to the larger fraud and extortion.

As the number of events increase around the world, corruption will be a greater issue for events, sponsors and authorities. This is simple linear analysis. There is copious information for mega events and sports events. When it does become an issue, there is little time to read up on all the international level information particularly for event with budgets under tens of millions of dollars. The references at the end of this can of course be consulted. But a concert or festival of 20,000 people does not have the same resources as the Olympics or World Cup. The information is excellent in these references, but it would be a struggle for the average event team to apply them to their event.

The stories in each chapter and the anecdotes are for illustration. They are quite real, but for obvious reasons most need to be anonymous. Nor are they an exhaustive survey of corruption in events. The corrupt are forever innovative in their methods and should be regarded as intelligent agents. They can read a book like this as well and adapt their techniques.

As this textbook takes a risk management approach, it is unrealistic to assume that all corruption will be eliminated. It will be there. A risk management approach is to minimise the likelihood and consequence. The aim "elimination of all corruption" may be laudatory and look good as a marketing statement, but it may obfuscate the realistic methods found in this book. To paraphrase the introduction to the *ISO 37001 Anti-Bribery Standard* (ISO, 2021):

Understanding and acting on the information in this textbook cannot provide assurance that no corruption has occurred or will occur in relation to the event, as it is not possible to completely eliminate the risk of corruption. However, this textbook can help the organization implement reasonable and proportionate measures designed to prevent, detect and respond to corruption.

A note to teachers and students

This textbook adapts the standard risk management process to the risk of corrupt practices in events and event planning. It should be part of any course on event management and within the risk management section. Although there is copious material on corruption in mega events and sports events, the rest of the events sector ignores this burgeoning issue. The teacher can use the case studies and ask the students to use the tools set out in Chapters 7 and 9 to analyse these examples and others that arise in the press. In the experience of the author, teaching and training around the world, the three analytic tools are particularly useful: scenarios, bowtie and causal analysis. Discussing, testing and refining the application of these tools ensure the students grasp that event management is complex, with multiple causes of risk and many amplifying factors.

The students should realise that field is dynamic and the corrupt are endlessly resourceful and they are free agents. They will respond and try to work around any solution that may be found. This is a secondary risk. Basically it is a cost benefit decision by the corrupt, i.e. is it worth the effort? By ensuring that the effort is not worth it, the event can minimise corrupt practices.

The fact that corruption is hidden is a new perspective on risk for students. Quite often students will only see immediate issues. Not only is it secretive, the negative effects may take years to become obvious. Even then, the link is hard to establish. To make it more difficult, the event is a project and once it is over, it basically disappears. This is unique and should provide plenty of thought for energetic discussion in class or workshop.

Summary

- ☐ Definition of corruption
- ☐ Corruption is worldwide
- ☐ As the event sector grows. so does the threat
- ☐ The book can be used as a manual, a training tool and for teaching

References

Australian Standards. (2001) *AS 8001-2021: Fraud and Corruption Control.* https://store.standards.org.au/reader/as-8001-2021

Graycar, A. (2015). Corruption: Classification and analysis, *Policy and Society* 34, 87–96

ISO (2021) *Whistleblowing Management Systems, ISO* 37002:2021. Switzerland: International Organization for Standardization.

Méon, P. & Weill, L. (2008). Is corruption an efficient grease?, *BOFIT Discussion Papers* 20, https://www.econstor.eu/

Nest, M. (2020). *Mining Awards Corruption Risk Assessment Tool.* 3rd ed. Transparency International. www.transparency.org.

Section 1

Events, Ethics and Corruption

מְעַלְלֵיהֶם יֵיטִיבוּ הָרַע כַּפַּיִם שֹׁפֵט שֹׁאֵל וְהַשֹּׁפֵט בַּשִּׁלּוּם דִּבְרוּ וְהַגָּדוֹל דֹּבֵר הַוַּת נַפְשׁוֹ הוּא וַיְעַבְּתוּהָ

"Both their hands are skilled in doing evil; the official and the judge ask for bribes, the powerful dictate what they desire— they all conspire together."

Old Testament Micah 7:3

ושוחד לא תקח כי השוחד יעור פקחים ויסלף דברי צדיקם

"And you shall take no bribe, for a bribe blinds the clear-sighted and subverts the cause of those who are in the right."

Torah Exodus 23:8

وَإِذَا تَوَلَّىٰ سَعَىٰ فِي الْأَرْضِ لِيُفْسِدَ فِيهَا وَيُهْلِكَ الْحَرْثَ وَالنَّسْلَ وَاللَّهُ لَا يُحِبُّ الْفَسَادَ

"And when he goes away, he strives throughout the land to cause corruption therein and destroy crops and animals. And Allah does not like corruption."

Koran Surah Al-Baqarah (2:205)

2 Why events?

The nature of events

The event sector is project based. Unlike sport, for example, it does not have centralised administration, such as FIFA or the IOC, to create the governance rules. The event associations are not able to enforce codes of conduct, except by expelling members. It is really a free for all type of industry. This is its attraction and source of its creativity. It is also its attraction for corrupt conduct.

There are various studies on the size of the event sector. But none of them are satisfactory for a worldwide view. Different types of events crop up all the time. Too often an assessment of the size and scope of the sector leaves out one part. Weddings, for example. An important event in many people's lives, worth billions of dollars around the world and yet not really covered by the general text-books on events. Religious celebrations and commemorations are not front of mind when thinking about the event sector. Tourism events receive plenty of press as do business events, such as conferences, and exhibitions. They are in the forefront of the minds of the innumerable visitor bureaus and the subject of economic impact studies around the world. Almost every sector from agricultural to finance has events such as conferences, exhibitions, seminars, festivals and concerts. This variety and spread is part of the attraction to the corrupt.

The millions of dollars involved in even the simplest event is enough to attract the criminal. A concert of 20,000 people is easily worth a minimum of two million dollars, simply worked out by the ticket price multiplied by the number of attendees. But this does not take into account the merchandise, food and beverage and sponsorship. On site there may be over a million dollars spent. When this was purely cash, the opportunities for criminal and corrupt behaviour were endless. With the credit cards, it has changed dramatically. Not extinguished, just moved into other areas of corruption.

Events are found around the world. Hence one form of corruption, such as money laundering, can take advantage of the cross border and touring events. There are a variety of opportunities for corrupt practices as the funds come and go from a number of sources. Merchandise, sponsorship, ticket sales, sale of assets, payment of suppliers, royalties and grants all make up this dynamic movement of money. It is more than the money that is dynamic as each event has a cluster of different suppliers. Even the regular supplier often had changed their staff from the last time they were contracted. The suppliers come and go, get bought out and go bankrupt. The stability needed for the prevention of corruption described in the UN and EU documents is just not found in many events.

The staff for event management, the planning and the event itself, can go from a few people to thousands. Recruitment is fast tracked and often the event will depend on volunteers. The recommendations in anti-corruption documents must be adapted to the 'pulsating' human resources. Many events such as public festivals are organised by non-profit entities often with a mixture of community groups and volunteers. These non-professionals have to negotiate and work with private companies with a strictly financial approach to the event. The number of stakeholders such as suppliers, sponsors and government entities, can create a mind boggling complexity of quick decisions with unexpected and uncertain outcomes. A seemingly small change in the logistics can have an overwhelming result. Hence a "small bit" of corruption to facilitate the flow of goods and services may seem a solution.

Within an organisation, such as a large company or bureaucracy, the event team, unit or department has a certain autonomy needed for the complexity of event management. This freedom can open the team to corruption. It can also create mini kingdoms within the larger organisation, engender favouritism and lead to fraud and the misappropriation of funds. The secrecy needed for negotiations, combined with the agility needed for last minute decisions, works to the favour of hidden and fraudulent behaviour.

It is the same with the local procedures, rules and regulations. They have been developed for ongoing governance and administration. The well-oiled standard methods are difficult to use and time consuming when time is short. It is well-nigh impossible to delay an event. It is time critical project management with a fixed deadline. A touring event has to face a myriad of new rules and regulations in each jurisdiction. A trade exhibition and promotion in Vladivostok faces completely different legal and cultural values to one in Chandigarh to one in Houston. The author was involved in all of these.

Figure 2.1 shows, in a bowtie diagram, the key contributing factors leading to corruption, and some of the many consequences that can arise from it. The contributing factors are listed on one side, and the consequences on the other, width corrupt practice being the knot in the middle of the bowtie.

It should be stressed that the event, such as an exhibition, concert or festival, is where the value is created. If the event is cancelled i.e. does not go ahead, then the work leading up to the event becomes a cost. Hence every aspect of the lead up to the event is evaluated with this in mind. In simple project management terms, the decisions are always: time /cost/quality. But the time for the event is its deadline. Any prevention of corruption strategy must be highly efficient. For events that are special or one off, there is no time for correction. A yearly event such as a local festival can incrementally correct itself each year. Their anti-corruption policy can improve. It can be tested and refined. Other events such as special events and touring events must have preventive policies that will work immediately. This is little or no time for correction and improvement.

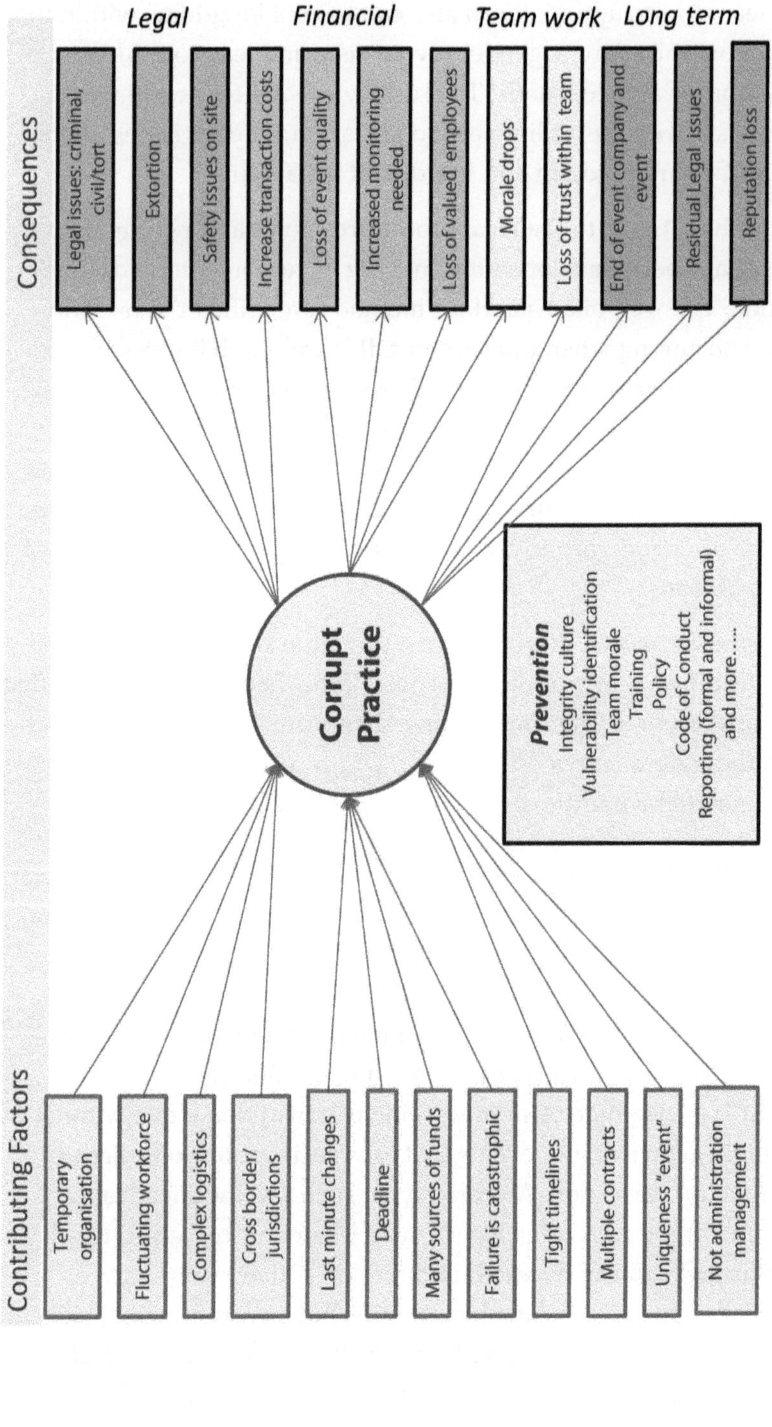

Figure 2.1: Simple Bowtie analysis of corruption and events

It is similar to the situation in sports as pointed out by the UN Global Compact Working Group Fighting Corruption in Sport Sponsorship and Hospitality

> *"Awareness of time-crunch snap decisions made for provision of products and services when an impending Sport Entity event deadline creates circumstances for business process safeguards (e.g., proper RFPs, due diligence background checks, conflicts of interests, contractual provisions) to be circumvented"*
>
> (UN Global Compact Working Group, 2014, p. 20)

This is stressed by the UN 2013 The United Nations Convention against Corruption A Strategy for Safeguarding against Corruption in Major Public Events:

> *"The exceptional nature of these events increases the likelihood that regulations and standard procedures might be relaxed or set aside. The shortness of time may make it difficult for existing monitoring, auditing and accountability mechanisms to effectively perform their function and have the desired impact. As a result, the necessary independent oversight of activities might be lacking and the allocation of public funds may not be transparent and subject to adequate controls."*
>
> (UN, 2013, p. x)

The pressure on the event team when there are changes may lead to expedient thinking, overriding rules and regulations and any warnings, in the hope that it will be "alright on the night". If the event is successful "all will be forgiven". Every time this happens, the hubris grows and the management is heading for a disaster. As is demonstrated in this textbook, the implications of corruption are wide, subtle and grow like a disease.

In an innovative industry there must be flexibility in authority and decision-making. Without this discretion, many events would never be fresh, new and probably never meet the deadline. This latitude in event planning and execution also creates potential for misconduct. The freedom to make quick decisions and allocate resources without constant oversight can be exploited by unethical individuals. This phenomenon is sometimes referred to as "*abuse of discretion*" (Graycar, 2013).

> *It is the forever tug of war between procedural compliance and adaptive problem solving.*

Events, such as public celebrations, concerts and festivals are dependent on publicity. It is vital as the event has to sell the product i.e. the event, long before the attendee experiences it. The event team is sensitive to any negative publicity leading up the event. An event tainted by corruption could easily fail financially. Hence there is a tendency to cover up corruption and deal with it internally – if at all.

A further risk the touring event has to face is the different cultures and attitudes to corruption. There are places where giving a service provider a personal reward is regarded as the only way to do business. The relationship between government and law varies across different countries and legal systems. While the Magna Carta originated in England and has had a significant influence on the UK's legal tradition, its principles have influenced many other countries' legal systems as well. The separation of powers and the rule of law are concepts that are implemented in various ways in different nations, with each country having its own unique legal framework and traditions.

The practice of tipping in the USA is an example. In other cultures ensuring your extended family members have a job is an important responsibility. Hence nepotism is not regarded with the same aversion around the world.

As pointed out in the Maturity Model of events sector development, the world is in the phase of the rule of the mega events. (O'Toole, 2022). They drive the laws, the standards, the training and the regulations. They attract vast amount of publicity and funding. These laws are not scalable but the smaller event still has to abide by all of them. The temptation to skirt the time consuming bureaucratic regulations by "greasing the wheels" is strong.

A contributing factor to this myriad of responsibilities and tasks is the politician. Events attract politicians. Then they are seen when people are celebrating or other important occasions, precisely because they are seen and associated with the celebration. The author has experienced this ranging from princes to government ministers to local politicians. In some cases they interfere in the planning, in other cases they just turn up on the day. Politicians can introduce many kinds of corruption including patronage, conflict of interest and a completely separate source of power, money and influence. The United Nations broadens this to Politically Exposed Persons (PEP). This is someone who holds a prominent public position in a government or international organisation. Through their position, they may have power and influence, and access to and control over money and resources (AUSTRAC, 2022). Hence they may have access to state funds and therefore represent a unique risk to the event.

Lastly, once the event has finished, it is difficult to trace and prove any past corruption. The event team and suppliers have dispersed, the event site cleaned and back to normal. Often they have moved on to different countries. There were so many decisions and last minute changes that tracking these is almost impossible. The cost can be prohibitive.

Story 1: Arresting

A police station in one city was inside the stadium precinct. There was a famous rap artist performing to a sold out audience in the stadium. Some members of the local police desperately wanted to see and hear this artist. Their solution was to arrest people outside the stadium. Then they are required to escort them to the nearest police station for charging. This was conveniently located in the stadium. Hence they were able to enjoy the concert without paying for entrance tickets.

The above section describes why the creating, developing and managing an event, be it a festival, celebration, product launch, concert or any other, does not directly fit with the various preventative measures outlined and described in the UN and other excellent documents and websites. Event management is dynamic, responding to changes and developments, often with a myriad of stakeholders and sponsors in a new area or site. All of this culminates in a few hours, a day or maybe three days of value creation. It then effectively disappears. Figure 2.1 uses one of the tools found in Chapter 10 to summarise all these points about the attraction of events.

This dynamism as will be seen over the various chapters also attracts corruption. Unfortunately, we can never know the extent of it as, by its very nature, corruption is hidden, in the dark.

The netherworld

It goes without saying that exposed corruption is only an indicator of the extent of corruption. There are too many interests to expose its spread and depth.

The information that is collected on corruption is recognised as only the 'tip of the iceberg'. But, with an iceberg, at least you can look under the water to see its size. It is impossible with corruption. The court cases in and out of the event domain, such as Bernie Madoff and Bankman-Fried, may indicate its spread and depth in just the finance sector. Again with corruption in customs and immigration, only the people caught will indicate its breadth and depth. Keep in mind that events cross all these sectors. It is the nature of these criminal actions that they are hidden. Petty crime such as small bribes will never be admitted and difficult to discover. There is no database. Any statistics must rely on opinion. Hence the famous Transparency International's Corruption Index is called the Corruption Perceptions Index (CPI) (Transparency International, 2021a).

Once people are compromised, they are open to extortion. A person's exposure can then be traded. As Beria supposedly said *"Show me the man and I'll find the crime"*. This is not data that can simply be collected, collated, and analysed. It is hidden, in the dark, it is the netherworld. We all know it is there. It forms the basis of stories, plays, films and novels. Look no further than Shakespeare, John Huston, Orson Welles, Scorsese, Kurosawa and Steinbeck. No amount of hypothesis and testing will uncover it all. No amount of in depth questioning or polling will find it. The border official who pockets the $100 note is not going to talk about it to a pollster.

Ultimately it depends on the ethics of the general population.

It is quite possible that many of the event disasters such as the stage collapse, crowd crush involved elements of corruption. Paying the security guard to look the other way while extra people are allowed into the venue, slipping the safety officer a bribe to ignore the expiring date on the slings can lead to the collapse of the gantry, hiring the less than competent relations of the manager to work on site will lower workforce capacity. When it happens there is no evidence and no one will expose it. Hence much of the day to day petty corruption remains hidden forever. It is hardly, if ever, mentioned in textbooks and standards on events and event safety. Only the big press items, such as the infamous Fyre festival in the Bahamas in 2017, get any mention or analysis.

But it builds up. Trust is diminished. To bribe one guard is similar to bribing a security company. To hire your family member as a favour to your uncle is the same as hiring all your friends. Step by step, it infects the whole management of the event. Rumours abound and the other staff and team members soon realise what is happening. They have the choice of leaving the team, becoming corrupt themselves, keeping quiet or exposing the corruption. The latter is fraught with danger. The corrupt may be subject to criminal charges, jail time and it may be much bigger than assumed. The reputation of the event and the event company will plummet and people will then lose their jobs. Who would want to take on that responsibility?

Story 2: Immoveable date

Perhaps the best and clearest explanation of corruption in the event sector is found in the Auditor General's Report on the 2010 Commonwealth Games in India. It is highly readable and covers almost all the corruption listed in this book. Although it concerns a major to mega event, it abounds with petty corruptions that are magnified by their repetition and, therefore, quite visible.

The quote below is an example of how this document focused on the factors of event management that make corruption a pathway for far too many people. In this case it is the pressure of 'time', combined with the risk of failure.

"The modus operandi observed over the entire gamut of activities leading to the conduct of the Games was: inexplicable delays in decision making, which put pressure on timelines and thereby led to the creation of an artificial or consciously created sense of urgency. Since the target date was immovable, such delays could only be overcome by seeking, and liberally granting, waivers in laid down governmental procedures. In doing so, contracting procedures became a very obvious casualty. Many contracts were then entertained based on single bids, and in fact, some of them were even awarded on nomination basis. Taking liberties with governmental procedures of the aforementioned kind led to elimination of competition."

(Auditor General, 2011, p.6).

This is called the corruption trap. Each act of petty corruption is self-reinforcing. The incentive to act corruptly increases as the corruption becomes common. It can become regarded as the only way to achieve results and therefore rational behaviour. Once it becomes normal it is difficult to escape. Its secrecy means that any open development in the event planning and the event is fraught with hidden traps.

For this reason the 'whistleblower' legislation enacted in many countries is relevant to the events sector. See Chapter 10, Governance, for more information.

The lack of trust in the event management can diminish their moral standing and therefore can be used by their competitors to their advantage. As pointed out in the United States Strategy on Countering Corruption 2021 (p.6), it also empowers enemies.

> *"Corruption also indirectly contributes to reduced public trust in state institutions, which in turn can add to the appeal of illiberal actors who exploit popular grievances for political advantage."*

The answer then is to realise it is a risk that has to be managed. In the first place the event has to be examined from this risk point of view. Where are the vulnerabilities? This is to reduce the likelihood of corruption called prevention.

Summary

The factors that contribute to exposure to corruption:

- ☐ Huge sums of money involved.
- ☐ Occur around the world in every industry sector.
- ☐ Variety of sources of money.
- ☐ Local procedures are made for administration management not time critical project management.
- ☐ Secrecy as to any corrupt dealing in case of negative publicity.
- ☐ Some cultures have corruption as part of everyday life.
- ☐ Difficult environment, time dependant decisions, last minute changes characterise by complexity and uncertainty.
- ☐ Temporary workforce often with rapid expansion of numbers.
- ☐ Autonomy needed for the events unit within a larger organisation.
- ☐ Mix of community, volunteers and private interests.
- ☐ Once the event has finished, it is difficult to trace and prove any past corruption.

Corruption

- ☐ By its very nature is hidden.
- ☐ Destroys trust and the team spirit
- ☐ Can lead to disasters at the event.

References

Auditor General. (2011). *Audit Report 2010 Commonwealth Games in India,* Comptroller and Auditor General of India, Union Government (Civil) Report No 6 of 2011-12. https://cag.gov.in/en/audit-report/details/2586

AUSTRAC. (2022). *Regulatory Quick Guide: Politically exposed persons.* https://www.austrac.gov.au/sites/default/files/2022-02/AUSTRAC_2022_PEPQuickGuide_web.pdf

Graycar, A. and Prenzler, T. (2013). *Understanding and Preventing Corruption.* Palgrave Macmillan.

O'Toole, W.J. (2022). *Events Feasibility and Development: from Strategy to Operations.* 2nd Edition, UK: Routledge

Transparency International. (2021a). *The ABCs of the CPI: How the corruption perceptions index is calculated.* https://www.transparency.org/en/news/how-cpi-scores-are-calculated

UN Global Compact Working Group. (2014). *Fighting Corruption in Sport Sponsorship and Hospitality: A practical guide for companies.* New York:United Nations. https://unglobalcompact.org/library/771

UN. (2013). *The United Nations Convention against Corruption: A Strategy for Safeguarding against Corruption in Major Public Events.* Vienna:UN.

United States Government (2103) *Strategy on Countering Corruption.* https://www.whitehouse.gov/wp-content/uploads/2021/12/United-States-Strategy-on-Countering-Corruption.pdf

3 Ethics

"Unless the LORD watches over the city, the watchmen stand guard in vain."

Psalm 127:1

This biblical quote carries profound implications beyond its religious context. In essence, it suggests that regardless of the number of systems, safeguards, and laws in place, the ultimate protection lies in the shared moral values of the people involved. This is reflected in contemporary anti-corruption papers which increasingly emphasize fostering 'integrity' rather than just focusing on preventing and detecting corrupt practices.

In the dynamic field of event management, this approach holds particular relevance. While robust systems and controls are necessary, cultivating a culture of integrity among all stakeholders can be far more effective in maintaining ethical standards. THE shift in focus from mere compliance to the promotion of ethical behaviour aligns well with the complex and fast-paced nature of event management where adaptability and trust are crucial.

Ultimately, corruption is wrong. It is that simple. But if we are discussing the minefield of ethics and morality in the modern world, we must describe why it is wrong. Here we get into a field that goes back to Aristotle's Ethics, flows through the rise of the worlds religion and cultures and is currently in the area of human rights. The Ancient Greek word was *phthora* meaning the gradual decay of something that was once good. We retain this meaning when we use it to describe food.

For example, corruption poses multiple challenges to governments, including significant loss of potential tax revenue. Corrupt payments, unlike every other aspect of finance must be hidden from the government. Therefore the loss in taxes as a result of corruption can only be guessed. It certainly one of the drivers of government interest in defeating it. One clear consequence is that honest citizens and businesses bear a disproportionate tax burden, as they effectively subsidize those engaging in corrupt practices. The flow of money and, in particular, the taxes, such as VAT or GST, are a source of information on economic health and a method to forecast future investments and development. The secrecy of corruption skews this information and devalues economic decisions. The long term effect is a sick economy.

Surveying the literature and thinking about corruption, the beginning chapters and paragraphs always start with the consequences of corruption. The two quotes below are typical examples.

> *"This document presents a policy statement on why anti-corruption is an issue of concern for investors, and explains how corruption is ultimately detrimental to investor value and financial performance"*
>
> (ICGN, 2020, p. 2)
>
> *"Today, corruption has moved away from its past rudimentary examination as an individual moral concept and is recognized as the main source of policy failure around the world."*
>
> (Pozsgai-Alvarez, 2020, p. 2)

This is **Consequential Ethics**. That an act or lack of action is wrong because it leads to an undesirable outcome. Hence these statements claim a cause to effect. Fortunately investor value and financial performance are measurable outcomes. What is policy failure? Against what is it measured?

The effect is described as undesirable and therefore the cause is wrong. This moves the definition and may lead to a circular definition. Undesired by whom? Is what is undesired by people the equivalent of it being wrong?

Regardless of the causal consistency of this type of thinking, it pervades all the writing on corruption from the United Nations down to the local government. Once it is pointed out, the reader can then frame the arguments about corruption. The ultimate 'undesirable ' is being sent to prison, i.e. guilty of a criminal offence. This means the effect must be traced to a crimes act, common law or another government act such as the Corporation Act. Extortion and money laundering are two types of corruption that are illegal. This may sound obvious, but there are many documents that muddy these ethical waters.

Gifts are a good example. We all give gifts, but when does this slide into a corrupt practice. This may seem a minor issue until the number of accusations and cases against the pharmaceutical industry and medical conferences are researched. Some of the recent cases include: Schering-Plough (now part of Merck & Co.) and the American College of Cardiology (ACC) conference, Purdue Pharma, the manufacturer of OxyContin and the Continuing Medical Education (CME) conferences and Biogen, a biotechnology company that manufactures the Alzheimer's disease drug, Aduhelm, and the sponsorship of medical conferences focused on neurology and Alzheimer's disease. These live in the grey zone where smart targeted marketing may be interpreted very differently.

Another example is **bribery** – is it a cultural expectation or just a tip? In some countries and cultures, you are expected to add 15% on top of the fee.

Of interest, in *Corruption Offences*, Lenny Roth (2013) describes the change from fee based service to salaries, i.e. fixed wages, over history. One can expand this further to societies where the person receiving the goods or service paid the person providing it directly. The USA custom of 'tipping' is an example of this. The waiter, for example, expects a direct payment from the customer that supplements their wage. It can be argued that wages and salaries arose out of the gradual industrialisation of societies. Societies that went from rural/feudal/tribal to modern in the space of 50 years are far more used to paying directly for a service. The creation of wages then combined with income taxes to create two economies. One is taxed and the other is cash. The next step was a 'goods and service' tax and the tipping economy became the black economy. Hence the concept of bribes is not as clear as the definitions assert.

One of the solutions to this complexity is to focus, not on preventing corruption, but promoting integrity. Needless to say, the term 'integrity' is fraught with many issues. However it does take a more positive view. The major issue with this ethical approach is that unless it is real it can lead to the opposite. What may be termed 'integrity washing' or 'integrity theatre'. This is using the words, creating an integrity framework and training the staff, but lacking any real operational implementation. It can lead to cynicism and heightened secrecy in the staff. (Maesschalck, 2008)

The economics of trust

Corruption such as bribery increases the transaction cost and this may be far more than the immediate money. It can be 'exposure' and lack of trust. From the asset management point of view, this is weakening the social capital. Social cohesion and the informal aspects of negotiation and general wellbeing are lessened by the lack of trust. The result is segregation within the event team into groups, those in the know and the others. All information during the event planning will now take extra time in verification. On-site information that is vital to active risk management may not be trusted. It leads to diminishing the creativity and innovation necessary for event management. The catastrophic risk of exposure is added to all the other risks in creating and managing the event. If the event team is suspected of corruption it will reduce willingness of companies to engage with the event. This leads to missing opportunities so necessary in the more creative end of the events sector. All of this can be seen as an extra cost to the event.

As illustrated in Figure 3.1, the **direct costs** of a lack of trust include transaction costs, contract enforcement costs, legal fees, reduction in business transactions and sponsorship, extra verification of information, extra security necessary and staff attrition.

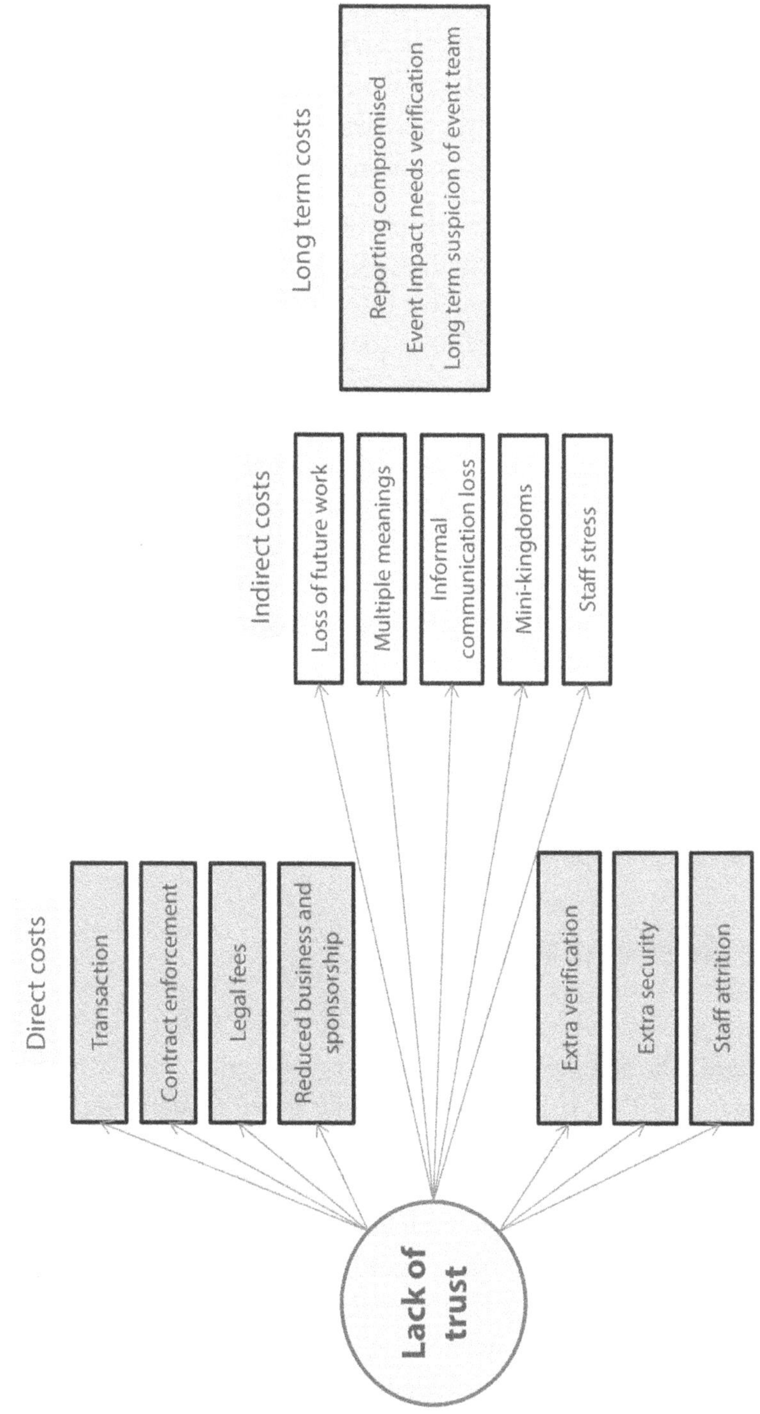

Figure 3.1: The cost of the lack of trust

Indirect costs include staff stress, secrecy, formation of mini kingdoms, reduced willingness to help, no informal channels of communication and team spirit, and any management communication has multiple meanings, shifting the risk to a later time and therefore creating a disaster that ends the event company or team.

The **long term result** of the loss of trust is found in the term the *Tragedy of the Commons*. The commons are shared resources in a community. This can be a tangible resource such as a park or swimming pool. Historically, the village common was a shared area of land to be used for grazing animals for anyone in the village community. It can also be extended to intangible resources such as a festival. The tragedy is that an individual can exploit the commons for their personal gain at the expense of the community. The result may be hidden at first. The long term result is the destruction of the commons. The individual – or group, walk away with their advantages and the community are left with the cost.

What can stop this? It takes more than a legal system, compliance and penalties. It takes common ethics and trust that everyone will follow it. The economics of trust is not simply a short term cost benefit analysis, it is a strategic plan intertwined with morality and personal ethics.

The descent into fraud

The Fyre Festival was a good example of the descent into fraud. The festival was to be a luxury weekend of music in the Bahamas in 2017. It collapsed financially and led to many legal actions. But, according to the court cases, the promoter didn't start out to defraud. It was the gradual move into fraudulent behaviour. It is similar to the gambler's curse: chasing. This is when the gambler keeps betting in order to cover their increasing losses. The losses get bigger, so they bet more money. When do you stop? What are the characteristic of this descent into fraud? How will you know? As pointed out by Eric Spengler, in his analysis of the Fyre Festival (Spengler, 2024), there is a pathway of fraud, to straight criminal fraud. In legal terms it can start with Negligent Misrepresentation or simply over-exaggerating the event and assuming a 'wish list' will come true. When financial matters become obviously a problem, the next step it to misrepresent the event in the hope it will all work out. The step now involves Unfair and Deceptive Trade Practices and Breach of Contract.

This is a common issue as events are often financially risky and occur over fixed period with the deadline that gives the value. If the event does not go ahead there can be a large financial loss and the waste of many months of hard work. It could also ruin the career of the event company. This means very different thinking to administration or ongoing management. People can quite often start with an 'innocent' view of managing an event and incrementally make decisions to find they have descended into illegality. In the author's experience the innocent view is very common as people assume event management is easy and extrapolate from their attendance at events. In the case of the descent into fraud, the intent to defraud or, *mens rea* in legal terms, is not there. It could be called stupidity or inexperience but it amounts to the same. Like a gambler trying to recover their loss by chasing. The lack of probability expertise in the average gambler cannot be used as an excuse for chasing.

Chasing, in the context of gambling, refers to the behaviour of continuing to wager money in an attempt to recover losses incurred during previous gambling sessions. It is a common phenomenon observed among gamblers who have experienced losses and feel compelled to keep playing in the hopes of recouping their money.

Chasing typically arises from various psychological factors, such as:

- **Loss aversion:** People tend to experience the pain of losses more intensely than the pleasure of gains. As a result, they may be motivated to take risks in an attempt to avoid or mitigate losses.

- **Gambler's fallacy:** This is the belief that past outcomes influence future outcomes in games of chance, even though each event is independent. For example, a gambler might believe that after a series of losses, a win is more likely to occur soon, which motivates them to keep playing.
- **Emotional attachment:** Gamblers may become emotionally invested in the outcome of their bets, particularly when significant amounts of money are at stake. This emotional attachment can cloud judgment and lead to impulsive decision-making.

If we apply this to events such as the Fyre festival it can follow a similar path. It starts with good intentions and a legitimate idea. Although there are early challenges, the optimism of the team overcomes these. It can include unexpected costs and low ticket sales. In response the promoter cuts a few aspects of the event. With their drive and optimism the event promoter sees the setback as a glitch. The staff reflects the promoter's thinking, reinforcing the promoter's actions. If viewed from the right perspective, all the financial projections look good.

At this point sponsors are concerned as ticket sales are not working out. Now the promoter starts to misrepresent the reality and leave out awkward figures. But there is a snowball effect such as lower ticket sales, artists withdrawing and sponsors demanding realistic figures. The promoter must come up with solutions. How can they leverage the sales that have already occurred? One way it to sell a cashless prepaid festival card. The extra money comes in before the event, but it is still not the amount needed for the artists, promotion, accommodation and all the other pre-event costs. At this point the promoter and the team know they are in trouble. It is a point of no return. But they must keep up the facade and hope for a miracle. They delay answers and further exaggerate the benefits. Team members start leaving.

The outcome of this descent into fraud can be that it is all discovered before the event, with the event being cancelled and possible legal repercussions. If the event does occur it would be nothing like what was advertised and have potential lawsuits. Another scenario, the promoter hopes there could be a last minute surge in ticket sales or a sponsor steps in to save the event. In this case the fraud would be covered up, forgotten and this is the hope of the promoter. But the promoter and complicit staff all committed fraud and they will never forget it. The promoter has not only used the Geryon, but introduced him to the events staff and he will not leave.

Story 3: Extravagance

Decadence: the Shah's party 1971 – consequence

To celebrate the 2500th anniversary of the formation of the Persian Empire, the then Shah of Iran decided to throw a party. This was no normal party as the heads of state of all the countries around the world were invited and it was to be held in the ancient capital of the Persian empire, Persepolis. The magnificent city had been destroyed with fire by Alexander the Great. There are a variety of estimates of the cost of the party. The minimum was over $100 million in today's money, the maximum was over five times that amount. The guest list included one Emperor, eleven Kings and Queens, twenty four Prince and Princesses, eighteen Presidents, an assortment of Dukes, Prime Ministers, one Sheikh, Emirs and one Sultan and many more. The extravagance was spectacular and possibly contributed to the downfall of the Shah a few years later. Corruption was one of the accusations against the Shah and the proof was the enormous cost of this party.

Exercise

1. Can a Shah be corrupt?
2. Is this an example of political corruption?
3. In this case the proof of corruption was the event. Was it in fact proof?
4. Research this event and discuss the implications of politicians using events to further their personal agenda in a modern democracy.

This scenario highlights how financial pressure, optimism bias, and the fear of failure can lead someone down a path of increasing dishonesty and fraud. It underscores the importance of realistic planning, transparent communication, and maintaining ethical standards in event organization.

For the purposes of event management the characteristics of a person who is chasing losses are similar as those open to corrupt practices. These include:

- **Neglecting responsibilities:** Chasing can lead to neglecting responsibilities at work or home in favour of finding the money. Someone who is chasing losses will prioritize income generation over other important commitments and obligations.
- **Borrowing money or financial problems:** Chasing losses can result in financial strain and difficulties. If someone is borrowing money frequently, experiencing financial problems, or exhibiting secretive behaviour regarding their finances, it may be a red flag for the person chasing losses.
- **Emotional distress:** Chasing losses can be emotionally distressing, leading to mood swings, irritability, anxiety, or depression. If someone appears to be experiencing heightened emotional distress, especially after any financial losses, it could be a sign of underlying chasing.
- **Denial or defensiveness:** Individuals who are chasing losses may deny or downplay the extent of their behaviour. They may become defensive when questioned about their promotion activities or finances.

The next story describes three cases of the descent. In the first two there is an innocence from the lack of experience, combined with an almost optimistic blindness to reality. Every event professional will know this type of person. But it should be remembered that they also attract people who are far more cunning and use the optimism for fraudulent behaviour. In the case of the Willi Wonka event the person was experienced. Story 3 could be seen as fraud on the world. Hubris on an international scale that led to a revolution and a realignment of geopolitics.

Story 4: Inexperience an excuse?

These three interesting stories have similarities to the infamous Fyre Festival.

The first is the 2018 TanaCon event that took place in Anaheim, California, at the Anaheim Marriott Suites. The event has copious information about it online including films, which is unsurprising as it was a YouTube themed event. It was for the fans of YouTube personality, Tana Mongeau, scheduled to run opposite the huge and well known VidCon event. The venue had capacity of 1500 pax and the estimates of the crowd numbers on the day varies from 5000 to 10,000. According to all the press and social media it was the mess that a professional event organiser would expect when seeing those figures. The event company eventually sued for bankruptcy.

The second example is more obvious as the organisers admitted they have never done this before. "*We are first timers and we intend to learn from our mistakes*" (Internet Historian, 2017). This is very common around the world. People assume what they see at an event is all they have to do to get an event together. The event was the 2014 Dashcon in Renaissance Schaumburg Convention Center Hotel in Schaumburg, Illinois – a fan event of Tumblr uses. 5000 people were expected and only 350 arrived. This meant very low ticket sales, low income, but the hotel hire remained the same. The hotel realised this was not working and demanded payment up front. The event organisers appealed for donation from the attendees. The facilities were not as expected by the audience, some of whom claimed they were scammed and there was corruption.

The third example is the Willy Wonka Experience described as a 'disaster' across the web. Whereas the first two examples are for adults, albeit young adults, the Willy Wonka Experience was for children. It was to take place in Glasgow in 2024. The promotion via social media was colourful and promised *"a celebration of chocolate in all its delightful forms".* On the day the people arrived to an almost empty warehouse with desultory decoration. They demanded their ticket money back. To quote one attendee *"This is where dreams come to die".* The organisers, the House of Illuminati, apologised and cancelled the event as people were arriving with their children. It was a failure. An interesting legal matter is the copyright issue. Did they get permission to use the well known books and film as the basis of their event. According to PlagiarismToday, they were sailing close to the wind. The name of the event was "Willy's Chocolate Experience" and the main character "Willy McDuff". The AI generated artwork and script were remarkably similar to the film and books, but the use of AI may have washed the original of copyright. We will never know. As they conclude:

"In the end, the thing that may best protect the organizers of the event is the fact that it was such an epic failure. If this had been a commercial and critical success, it is highly likely that various rights holders would have come out of the woodwork to demand their cut but, as a financial failure mocked widely online, I doubt that any will be so bothered." (PlagiarismToday, 2024).

Exercise

These three events have films about them online and make a good comparison.

1. Was there 'descent into fraud'?
2. Did it all start with innocence and gradually "chase" into negligence and fraud.
3. When was the 'point of no return'?
4. Is it the case of Hanlon's razor : Never attribute to malice that which can be adequately explained by stupidity?

Summary

- ☐ Corruption is morally wrong.
- ☐ Consequential ethics examines the undesirable outcomes.
- ☐ Not all corruption is criminal.
- ☐ The loss of trust has direct economic and social consequences.
- ☐ In events a company or solo promoter may start with the best intention but descend into fraud.
- ☐ Descent into fraud is similar to the consequence of chasing.

References

ICGN. (2020). *Guidance on Anti-Corruption Practices*. UK :International Corporate Governance Network. https://www.icgn.org/

Internet Historian. (2017). *The Failure of Dashcon | The world's first Tumblr convention*. https://youtu.be/1ZgxeX2dCnQ?t=339

PlagiarismToday. (2024). *Copyright, Trademark and Willy's Chocolate Experience*. https://www.plagiarismtoday.com/2024/03/04/copyright-trademark-and-willys-chocolate-experience/

Pozsgai-Alvarez, J. (2020). The abuse of entrusted power for private gain: meaning, nature and theoretical evolution. *Crime, Law and Social Change*, 74 (4), 433-455. DOI: 10.1007/s10611-020-09903-4.

Roth, L. (2013). *Corruption offences*. NSW Parliamentary Research Service, https://www.parliament.nsw.gov.au/researchpapers/Documents/corruption-offences/corruption%20offences.pdf

Spengler, E. (2024). *Fraud and the Fyre Festival Part 1: A Legal Analysis of the World's Worst Music Festival*. https://www.sab.law/news-and-insights/blog/fyre-festival-fraud-music-billy-mcfadden-illegal-sue

Section 2

Types of Corruption

"מְעַלְלֵיהֶם יֵיטִיבוּ הָרַע כַּפֵּי שֹׁפֵט שֹׁאֵל וְהַשֹּׁפֵט בַּשִּׁלּוּם דִּבְּרוּ וְהַגָּדוֹל דֹּבֵר הַוַּת נַפְשׁוֹ הוּא וַיְעַבְּתוּהָ"

Both their hands are skilled in doing evil; the official and the judge ask for bribes, the powerful dictate what they desire— they all conspire together.

Old Testament, Micah 7:3

Μὴ πλανᾶσθε· φθείρουσιν ἤθη χρηστὰ ὁμιλίαι κακαί.

"Do not be deceived: 'Bad company corrupts good character.'"

Bible 1 Corinthians 15:33

குறள் 284: களவின்கண் கன்றிய காதல் விளைவின்கண்
வீயா விழுமம் தரும்.

The lust inveterate of fraudful gain, Yields as its fruit undying pain.

The Tirukkuṟaḷ, Kura 204, Tamil 4th BC

The first step in the analysis of corrupt behaviour in order to minimise its occurrence is to divide the practices into categories.

In their online *Corruptionary*, Transparency International (Transparency International, 2022a) subdivides corruption into three types: petty, grand and political corruption. Their definitions are concerned with public officials, however it can be expanded to anyone with authority.

- **Petty corruption** is the everyday misuse of entrusted power by officials during their interactions with ordinary citizens, often when these citizens are trying to access essential goods or services in places such as hospitals, schools, police departments, and other agencies. An example is having to pay the border guard to exit a country or paying the site manager a 'tip' to get the best position for your stall at a festival.
- **Grand corruption** is the exploitation of high-level authority that benefits a select few at the expense of the many, causing significant and widespread harm to individuals and society as a whole. Using the event economy to launder drug money is an example of this. Selling the private details of the attendees is another example.
- **Political corruption** the manipulation of policies, institutions, and procedural rules in the allocation of resources and financing by political decision-makers, who exploit their positions to maintain their power, status, and wealth. It mostly concerns mega events, although on a local level it can include funding a politician with the understanding they 'assist' the event in the legal processes or ensuring family members have priority for important paid positions in the organising committee.

It is the theme of this book that the petty corruption has a pervading and damaging effect on events and provides the raison d'etre for the mega corruption that we hear so much about.

These examples illustrate how different types of corruption manifest in various contexts, highlighting the pervasive and damaging effects of corrupt practices on society.

All three are present in the events sector. They are all related. Petty corruption provides the culture to enable grand and political corruption. It rots the integrity expected of politicians and industry leaders. Petty is probably the wrong name for it. This supposed small time corruption in the event context can lead to disasters at the event. Unfortunately this type of the corruption is the easiest to hide and therefore society only knows about it through their community interactions.

The following describes nine types of corruption. All of them are found in the events sector. The illustrative stories are all true. They have been changed to ensure anonymity, but the core of the description remains the same. It is only the major or grand corruption that is public and often exposed in the press. Major event failures such as stage collapse or crowd crush may be traced back to corrupt practices. But this enters the secret world of bribery and collusion. Similar to all disasters, the people responsible will start "distancing". This means they place as much information distance between their actions and the disaster. Petty corruption is almost impossible to investigate as the resources required to catch the person are not commensurate with the results. However, as stressed in this book, petty corruption may form the foundation to major corruption. A person giving or taking a small bribe is hardly surprised when a politician is paid to give preferential treatment to a supplier.

The techniques to minimise petty corruption are found in Chapters 8, 9 and 10.

Professor Graycar in his article *Corruption: Classification and analysis* (Graycar, 2015) introduced the helpful framework: types, activities, sectors and places (TASP) to analyse, classify and deal with corruption. As events are project based, I would add an extra dimension of time. There are certain times over the event project that are particularly vulnerable to corrupt practice. Table 1 gives the explanation. This is also a good teaching and training tool.

Table 1: Five dimensions of corruption derived from Prof. Adam Graycar

Type of corrupt behaviour.
What activity/task has been corrupted?
The area of management the corruption occurred.
The place where it occurred.
In what phase of the event project did it occur.

The next three chapters describe the types of corruption found in the events sector around the world. Each chapter has examples. Some are taken from legal records and others are press reports. It is well to keep in mind that petty corruption is hidden. Everyone involved will deny it. It is only when it is cumulative and makes a difference to the power and tax income of the government that the public will hear about it. Other stories come from people who have been disadvantaged by corruption, such as facilitation payments.

4 Bribery

Perhaps the most direct type of corruption is bribery. There is no data on the extent of it, except people's opinions and speculation. Secrecy is the very nature of bribery. An all-encompassing definition of bribery is found in the Anti-bribery Management Systems of the International Standards Organisation:

> *"3.1 bribery:*
> *offering, promising, giving, accepting or soliciting of an undue advantage of any value (which could be financial or non-financial), directly or indirectly, and irrespective of location(s), in violation of applicable law, as an inducement or reward for a person acting or refraining from acting in relation to the performance of that person's duties"*
>
> (ISO, 2016, p.2)

Table 4.1: Bribery transaction characteristics

Intent: both parties must know they derive benefit from the transaction.

Opportunity: It is done in secrecy without other members of the staff seeing it happening and generally at a point of constraint or where a decision must be make that permits an action.

Benefit: there must be a benefit to both parties.

Consequence: there can be unintended consequences that expose the act of bribery. Hence both parties must consider these. For example for the customs official, this extra cash may show up in their life style.

Colloquially, it is to offer money or favours to an official to misuse their authority. Secretly paying a customs and immigration official to expedite the passage of a performer into the country is an example of petty bribery. Understanding the characteristics of the transaction will help in minimising its occurrence. Table 4.1 lists these.

Each of these characteristics can be used to expose the two parties to the transaction. But far more important, in the fluid and complex management of events is to use the characteristics to prevent bribery in the first place.

Bribery in sport is very well described in the publications and websites such as the excellent documents written by the International Partnership Against Corruption in Sport (IPACS). The recorded examples of corruption in sport are worldwide and extend over history from the time of the ancient Greeks. The aim of most corruption in sport competitions is to remove the element of chance. According to IPACS there are three types of bribery:

- competition manipulation such as match fixing,
- concealing doping, and
- bribery to do with the management of the sport.

For the purpose of events, each of these may be considered if there are competitions of any kind as part of the event program. The international gambling that is found in sports is not found in events. As 'chance' does not play a large part in events, many of the types of sports corruption are not as important.

Grooming

When a member of the event team or volunteer accepts a bribe it opens them to extortion. The first bribe leads to other bribes which then compromises the staff member who is extorted. Hence a simple small payment can be leveraged to a major criminal act. To illustrate this. At a festival, the parking volunteer is slipped an undercover payment to allow a member of the pubic to park their car, just for 10 minutes. The next day the person asks again for that space, the volunteer parking attendant refuses, so the person ups the amount. The volunteer agrees. The next day, the same situation, but the volunteer refuses. The person then threatens to tell the event organises that the volunteer is accepting bribes. This time the volunteer agrees. This is called 'grooming' and the event team and volunteers must understand that a bribe is not a stand-alone occurrence; it may rapidly lead far worse situations.

Grooming, in this context, refers to the calculated approach of targeting people with authority. It involves the intentional manipulation by individuals, whether they're part of an organization or not, with the aim of identifying and exploiting this insider. The ultimate goal is to enable or expand fraudulent or corrupt activities. Those who engage in grooming dedicate significant effort to understanding their potential targets. They use various tactics to manipulate, pressure, or extort these individuals to achieve their corrupt objectives. To illustrate the secrecy involved in corruption there is a specialist terminology, prison slang, in gaols for grooming, the target is called a 'duck' and the practice of gradually manipulating them with simple requests or small bribes until they can be extorted is called 'ducking'.

Ashurst, the British multinational law firm headquartered in London, makes the observation that the customs and practice of another country are no defence against the charge of bribery. This is important for any event company that works around the world. They stress the term 'intention to influence' does not mean there is a specific objective. For example the influence may be to show favour in a future action. They state:

> *"Courts infer an intention to influence from all the circumstances in which the benefit is given e.g. the size of the benefit(s), the frequency of benefit(s), the context (e.g. if there was an impending decision regarding e.g. the grant of a licence or award of a contract), and whether the benefit was recorded by either party and recorded accurately."*
>
> (Ashurst, 2022).

The UN Global Compact Working Group comprehensively defines bribery and subdivides it:

- ***Bribery***: *This is the offering, promising, giving, accepting, or soliciting of an advantage as an inducement for an action, which is illegal, unethical, or a breach of trust or to refrain from acting. Bribery can be a financial or in-kind undue advantage that can be paid directly or through intermediaries. The enterprise should consider the most prevalent forms of bribery in its risk assessment, including kickbacks, facilitation payments, gifts, hospitality, expenses, political and charitable contributions, sponsorships, and promotional expenses. Brief descriptions of some of these risks are given below:*
- ***Kickbacks***: *These are bribes fulfilled after an enterprise has awarded a contract to a customer. They take place in purchasing, contracting, or other departments responsible for decisions to award contracts. The supplier provides the bribe by kicking part of the contract fee back to the buyer, either directly or through an intermediary.*
- ***Facilitation payments***: *These are typically small payments made to secure or expedite the performance of a routine or necessary action to which the payer is entitled, legally or otherwise. They present concerns for entities as often payments are extorted in circumstances such as obtaining release of perishable goods from customs or seeking entry at the immigration desk.*
- ***Charitable and political donations, sponsorship, travel, and promotional expenses***: *These are legitimate activities for entities but can be abused by being used as a subterfuge for bribery. It should be noted that under the foreign bribery offences of many countries (in particular countries that are Party to the OECD Anti-Bribery Convention), there are risks attached to such transactions where it could be judged that an advantage has been given to a Foreign Public Official to obtain or retain business. "*

(Global Compact Working Group, 2013, p. 12)

Story 5: Bribery at the door

There are many reports of security guards taking bribes and allowing people into the venue. Given the number of events around the world and the new security requirements over the last few years, the temporary and rapidly trained staff and the level of wages, it should come as no surprise. This has reportedly lead to the death of patrons in the resulting crowd crush. For example:

"2 were killed in a crush after hundreds of fans without tickets were allegedly let in to see the Nigerian star Asake at the O2 Brixton Academy on this day last year".

Exercise

The sudden increase in the official requirement for security after the many attacks on events and festivals is an interesting study in risk. Here the proposed solution created other problems. New companies were created with little experience in events. The security was so ineffective that it was termed *"security theatre"*.

Research this on the web.

Although there are plenty of reports there is very little follow-up. Is this because private arrangements have been made?

There can be no doubt that events, particularly major events, touring events and tourism events will need a code of conduct and policy on bribery. The Bribery Act 2010 UK :

> *"The Act creates a new offence under section 7 which can be committed by commercial organisations which fail to prevent persons associated with them from committing bribery on their behalf. It is a full defence for an organisation to prove that despite a particular case of bribery it nevertheless had adequate procedures in place to prevent persons associated with it from bribing."*

(Ministry of Justice, 2011, p.7).

For the event team this implies their organisation or company, although temporary, is required to prove they have adequate procedures in place, not just for their staff and volunteers, but also for "persons associated". This may be taken to mean the myriad of suppliers and other temporary personnel. How far this will extend remains to be seen. The Appendix and Chapter 10 have templates for this looming issue for events and governments who host events.

Gifts and hospitality

It is very common to give gifts in events around the world, and gifts can take many forms. It can include souvenirs, hospitality, travel costs, donations, memberships and, the very common one, tickets to the event itself. From concerts to festivals to conferences, gifts are common. The distinction between an innocent gift and a bribe is about the intention. Even this is not at all clear as the intention is not obvious. Often the corrupt gift giver uses this ambiguity to deny it is a bribe. Even if there was no result, the gift can still be regarded as a bribe. As pointed out in the Hong Kong Prevention of Bribery Ordinance (PBO),

> *"as long as the offeror believes that the advantage given is a reward for favours done for him in business dealings, an offence is committed even if the recipient of the bribe has not eventually offered any assistance."*
>
> (Hong Kong, 2023)

Here it should be emphasised that there are two parties, the giver of the gift (offeror) and the receiver. With private events such as weddings, gifts are expected. With many events tipping can be construed as a gift. With public events it is the value of the gift that is used to evaluate if it is a corrupt practice. The general advice such as from the ISO 37001 is to steer clear of gifts that can be misconstrued as bribes, even if both parties are well intentioned. Larger events and annual events may have a clear written policy on gifts. It may include criteria such as the market value of gifts that can be given or accepted, the need to report all gifts immediately, or to seek approval in advance of accepting or giving gifts.

Story 6: Diwali gifts

The Indian Gudjarat Anti-Corruption Bureau (ACB), for example, warns about the yearly Diwali festival. The "Festival of Lights" celebrates the victory of light over darkness, good over evil, and knowledge over ignorance. An interesting irony is that it can also be a cover for bribing officials. According to the ACB, the gifts to the government officials can include cash, air tickets and luxury accommodation abroad. This is beyond the traditional gifts of a silver coins embossed with images of deities and traditional Indian sweets.

https://timesofindia.indiatimes.com/india/diwali-gifting-a-form-of-bribe-says-gujarat-acb-asks-officials-to-stay-clear/articleshow/87263298.cms

Once again the sports world is far in advance of the event sector on this issue. An example of this is the Anti-Bribery Policy of World Sailing:

> *"All gifts and benefits (including hospitality or entertainment) given or received by World Sailing employees, Board members and Associated Persons of a value in excess of £250 arising from or connected with employment at the World Sailing or actions taken in behalf of the World Sailing must be notified in writing to the Anti-Bribery Compliance Officer with 7 days of the receipt of the gift or benefit. The Anti-Bribery Compliance Officer will record it in the Register of Gifts."*
>
> (World Sailing, 2024).

Similar to World Sailing, numerous large event-sponsoring companies maintain guidelines on gifts. Government organising committees most certainly will have a policy as it is too close to bribery. A seemingly small gift may lead to extortion and further favours. The potential receiver should always ask why they are receiving a gift.

This can be a cross-cultural issue. In some countries gifts are expected and it is an insult not to come forward with a gift of a certain value. For example the Φακελάκι (*Fakelaki,* "little envelope") in Greece and the complexities of reciprocal gift giving in Japan. As gift giving and receiving often falls into the border zone or the grey area of legality and corruption, there are no end of stories in the media. Festivals, where giving a gift is part of the event, can easily be a cover for buying influence.

Story 7: Chinese Mooncake Festival

In Chinese mandarin the word is *guanxi* (关系) – local influence – and an event that provides an opportunity to increase a person's guanxi is the Mooncake Festival. It goes back over 3,000 years to the Zhou Dynasty. It was a time to give thanks for the harvest and to pray for future bounty. The Mooncake is the symbol of the event and it is a time for family reunions and offerings. Unfortunately the offerings can also be a cover for very expensive mooncake gift baskets and banquets given to local government officials, according to the Central Commission for Discipline Inspection (CCDI). The CCDI set up a website, an app and an account on Wechat to entice people to report on gatherings, banquets, sponsored tours and bribes accepted by government officials during the festival.

The two examples mentioned above demonstrate that when seemingly minor instances of bribery associated with widely celebrated events across cities and towns are aggregated, they can result in significant corruption and have a substantial impact on society. Individually, the instances of gift-giving might seem trivial. However the Indian Gudjarat Anti-Corruption Bureau (ACB), and Chinese Central Commission for Discipline Inspection (CCDI) realise the cumulative and pervasive effect on trust, governance and social capital. The mega events are far more centralised and therefore the instances of corruption can be spectacular and involve international players. But the effect, and possibly the amount, may well be dwarfed by the secret petty corruption found in the myriad of smaller festivals held around the country. The next example illustrates the spectacular corruption associated with a mega event.

Story 8: BHP Olympic payment

In 2015 the USA Securities and Exchange Commission charged the global resources company BHP Billiton with violating the Foreign Corrupt Practices Act (FCPA). As a result of this action BHP Billiton agreed to pay a $25 million penalty to settle the SEC's charges. Andrew Ceresney, Director of the SEC's Division of Enforcement asserted that:

"BHP Billiton footed the bill for foreign government officials to attend the Olympics while they were in a position to help the company with its business or regulatory endeavors. BHP Billiton recognized that inviting government officials to the Olympics created a heightened risk of violating anti-corruption laws, yet the company failed to implement sufficient internal controls to address that heightened risk."

Using the USA Foreign Corrupt Practices Act (FCPA), the SEC was able to bring BHP to court. The "*SEC Charges BHP Billiton With Violating FCPA at Olympic Games*" press release succinctly covers a number of failings.

"Although BHP Billiton put some internal controls in place around its Olympic hospitality program, the company failed to provide adequate training to its employees and did not implement procedures to ensure meaningful preparation, review, and approval of the invitations."

Two aspects of the case worth nothing: BHP Billiton is not a USA company and the charge related to an event seven years previously, the Chinese 2008 Olympics. (SEC, 2015a)

Exercise

The above story indicates a reference to 'tick boxing'. Discuss this risk in event planning. It is very common as more and more compliance is mandatory.

The entourage

A form of corruption is leveraging the hospitality of events. Accompanying personnel are the people who arrive with the main act. It could be a speaker at a conference bringing their partner or a band bringing their friends and relations. The other term for it is 'entourage'. If it is not covered in the contracts it can come as a surprise to the event team. They will now need to find accommodation, meals and transport. It is a form of extortion as the star knows the cost of cancelling far outweights the cost of the entourage. Unfortunately it is in the grey or border zone of negotiation, where the event team needs to be adaptable and yet strict with the conditions.

Story 9: Medicine

As a result of an investigation by the USA Securities and Exchange Commission the US based company 3M had to pay over $6 million USD. The charges were that they violated the provisions of the Foreign Corrupt Practices Act (FCPA). Its China subsidiary:

"arranged for Chinese health care officials to attend overseas conferences, educational events, and health care facility visits ostensibly as part of its marketing and outreach efforts, but that in fact were often a pretext to provide overseas travel, sightseeing and entertainment."

(SEC, 2023).

These were described as Educational Events delivered in English. According to the SEC report, one clue was that none of the Chinese delegates could speak English.

To finish the section on gifts and hospitality we can turn to the copious standards and codes in the Sports sector. Corruption in the sports sector, in terms of hospitality, sponsors expectations of free tickets and other gifts is well known. For this reason the UN has published *"Fighting Corruption in Sport Sponsorship and Hospitality: A practical guide for companies"*. Their recommendations for assessing hospitality can be directly transferred to events. Gifts and other hospitality should be made in the open and not have any obligation for future actions. Both sides should be quite willing to discuss the hospitality with other members of the team and other event stakeholders. The value of the hospitality should be reasonable when measured by the standards in that part of the events sector. It must be legal and not involve family members. It should not include cash payments.

There should be no obligation on the part of either party.
The offer should be openly made.
All the other event stakeholders should see the hospitality as reasonable.
The total value of the hospitality should be of reasonable value in the type of event.
It should be appropriate to the standards of the events.
It must be legal.
It must meet the standard of the recipient, such as their code of conduct.
It should be infrequent.
There should be no cash payments.
It should not be extended to the recipient's friends or family members.

Table 3: Assessing hospitality checklist adapted from UN Global Compact Working Group, 2014.

Story 10: More Medicine

According to the USA Department of Justice website:

"Between 2012 and 2015, Novartis Greece conspired with others to violate the FCPA by engaging in a scheme to bribe employees of state-owned and state-controlled hospitals and clinics in Greece in order to increase the sale of Novartis-branded pharmaceutical products. Novartis Greece paid for those employees to travel to international medical congresses, including events held in the United States, as a means to bribe these officials in exchange for increasing the number of prescriptions they wrote for Lucentis, a prescription drug that Novartis Greece sold. Novartis Greece employees traveled to the United States facilitated the provision of the improper benefits to publicly employed Greek health care providers." (DOJ, 2020)

Exercise

Here the company used events as a cover for gifts as well as gifts themselves. This also involves a whistleblower, an employee who wore a wire to record his conversations. He is due to be paid 18% of the over $300 million fine to be paid to the USA government by the company.

Research this case and discuss the implications for uncovering bribery.

Is rewarding the whistleblower with a percentage of the fine the best way to do this?

Summary

- ☐ Bribery definition ISO 37001:2016
- ☐ Characteristics: Intent, opportunity, benefit, consequence
- ☐ Grooming/duck
- ☐ Kickbacks, facilitation payments, charitable and political donations, sponsorship, travel, and promotional expenses
- ☐ The Bribery Act 2010 UK
- ☐ Assessing hospitality checklist
- ☐ Stories: Security, Diwali, Mooncake, BHP, pharmaceutical companies

References

Ashurst. (2022). *Anti-Bribery laws in Australia.* https://www.ashurst.com/en/insights/anti-bribery-laws-in-australia/

DOJ. (2020). *Novartis AG and Subsidiaries to Pay $345 Million to Resolve Foreign Corrupt Practices Act Cases.* www.justice.gov/usao-nj/pr/novartis-ag-and-subsidiaries-pay-345-million-resolve-foreign-corrupt-practices-act-cases

Hong Kong. (2023). *Prevention of Bribery Ordinance as at 2023.*CAP 201. https://www.elegislation.gov.hk/hk/cap201

ISO (2016). *Anti-bribery management systems — Requirements with guidance for use,* ISO 37001:2016. International Organization for Standardization

Ministry of Justice. (2011). *The Bribery Act 2010 Guidance.* UK:Ministry of Justice. www.justice.gov.uk/guidance/bribery.htm

SEC. (2015). *SEC Charges BHP Billiton with Violating FCPA at Olympic Games.* https://www.sec.gov/news/press-release/2015-93

SEC. (2023). *Administrative Proceeding File* No. 3-21581, https://www.sec.gov/files/litigation/admin/2023/34-98222.pdf

UN Global Compact Working Group. (2013). *A Guide for Anti-Corruption Risk Assessment.* New York:United Nations. https://unglobalcompact.org/library/411

World Sailing. (2024). *World Sailing Anti-Bribery Policy.* www.sailing.org/tools/documents/WorldSailingAntiBriberyPolicy-%5B23533%5D.pdf

5 Fraud

"It is an opportunistic infection that bursts forth when greed meets the possibility of deception."

(Silverstone et al., 2012, p. 12)

Introduction

Fraud, it may be argued is the most common form of corruption in events. It is as easy as telling a lie. If the event is a success, so many people believe, all is forgiven. The lies are forgotten and we move on to the next event. But luck is not the same as forgiveness. Eventually the Geryon will be obvious.

Fraud: "Any illegal act characterized by deceit, concealment, or violation of trust. These acts are not dependent upon the threat of violence or physical force. Frauds are perpetrated by parties and organizations to obtain money, property, or services; to avoid payment or loss of services; or to secure personal or business advantage."

(Office of the City Auditor, 2021)

According to Transparency International's The Anti-Corruption Plain Language Guide, fraud:

"is to cheat. The act of intentionally deceiving someone in order to gain an unfair or illegal advantage (financial, political or otherwise). Countries consider such offences to be criminal or a violation of civil law."

(Transparency International, 2009).

Many of the primary documents used to develop this manual have the term "corruption and fraud". This is because the current definition of corruption has the term "entrusted power" which, to the United Nations, implies government or corporate authority. This book on the other hand uses corruption in the more common usage and hence includes fraud, in the event context, as a form of corruption.

As set out in this chapter there are many forms of fraud at events. The main ones are: fraud in the promotion of the event, fraud in the event finances and ticketing fraud. The detailed exploration of vendor fraud was a result of my recent work on major festivals. Just as with the Rio example, I asked a few people who sold goods if they underreported sales at a festival. "Of course" was their reply, "Everyone does it". When everyone does it, it is the honest vendors who are disadvantaged. It inevitably evolves into dishonesty by other vendors and the overall loss of trust in other areas. How can these vendors trust their suppliers?

Described in Chapter 3, *The Economics of Trust,* this is a cost to all. Vendor fraud in these events, such as the ones I consulted to, was on a large scale. It involved attendees of over a million people over many weeks and the vendors include high class restaurants, specially built for the event. It was impossible to get the exact figures. My position was to find a solution for the future, not penalise those of the past. However it is a good case study for preventing corruption as there were many 'solutions' and the one I recommended was based on integrity and trust, through partnering.

Ticketing fraud has gone from photocopying the ticket, hoping no one notices, to a criminal enterprise. The various forms of ticket fraud are explored.

The chapter concludeS with an examination of collusion. An issue with bidding and major events. Similar to the conflict of interest and nepotism, we have to be careful of a practice that may be corrupt in the mega international events but has advantages in smaller events.

We will start this section with the most common issue and one we have all experienced: Marketing fraud.

Story 11: Event didn't exist

Two entrepreneurs convinced an investor to hand over a million and a half dollars to produce a music event that they knew would never happen.

"Morris and Kelly created several false and fraudulent concert performance contracts forging the signatures of the music recording artists. Morris also created false and fraudulent email accounts that he used to pose as if the music recording artists themselves had sent the signed contracts to Kelly and himself. Additionally, during a video call with the victim, Morris and Kelly had an accomplice pose as J.B. to trick the victim into believing that J.B. had agreed to perform at the concert series." (DOJ, 2024)

Marketing, fraud?

A person can't simply test or simulate the event experience. It must be felt viscerally, engaging all the senses. Being there, in the moment, is the very essence of what defines an event. The firsthand nature of participation is what makes each event unique and powerful. Compare this to any other purchased product. A person can look and feel it in a shop, or ask their friends if the product works. The point of an event is its fleeting nature. This may seem obvious, but it is too often missed by textbooks and theories. It is seen as a product and the attendees are customers as though it is in the same league as a washing machine or trip to the beach.

The fleeting nature of the event means the event team must convince the future attendee to pay and come to something they won't experience until they have done it. This unique experience is exactly what they are paying for. In the music sector, the event organisers were called 'promoters' as much of their time was selling the event experience to people.

Story 12: Camel beauty contest and botoxing the camels

The beauty contest with its huge prizes and future endorsements, where the winner can look forward to fame and fortune are a prime target for corruption. There a multiple stories in the press from around the world. No country seems to be excluded. Perhaps the most interesting occurred at the King Abdulaziz Camel Festival in Saudi Arabia. With prizes totalling over 50 million US dollars, the festival organisers had to be on guard. In 2021 at one of the events, the Camel Beauty Contest, 12 camels were disqualified after they were found to have botoxed lips. The size and beauty of the lips is one of the criteria in judging the beauty of a camel. The winner of this completion can fetch millions of dollars at the final auction.

It is because of this that many events move into the border zone between truth and lies. So much depends on attracting the audience, that exaggeration of the benefits can easily get out of hand. The Chinese call it *the border area* 界地带, *Jiè dìdài*. It is the indistinct zone between legal and illegal acts. An illustrative case is the distinction between fraud and marketing. One of the aims of marketing an event is to make it attractive as possible to the potential audience. Often the benefits are exaggerated into this border zone, between lies and the truth. The consequence of this has been obvious worldwide when far too many people arrive at the event. When this is expected due to prior ticket sales, the crowd security and ticketed entrance may not be an issue. However a free event, such as a store promotion can lead to pandemonium. This is a regular issue as described in Story 4 *Inexperience an excuse?* (p. 35) and Story 25 *Chaotic* (p. 129).

It is here we enter the world of the Geryon or fraud.

Story 13: Exorbitant

One of the foreign companies hired for the Commonwealth Games in India, according to the post-event investigation by the Auditor General, displayed many of the types of fraud found in this section. These include:

- ☐ Charging for executive personnel on a per month basis to be in India when one did not go to India.
- ☐ Charging for hired audio equipment that was never delivered.
- ☐ "Exorbitant" rates for hiring this company.
- ☐ Single bids made to the 'Fast Track Committee'.

"Audio video equipment for sports presentations were hired at exorbitant rates, through a highly flawed process. Our enquiries revealed that the quoted prices for purchase of the same equipment was about half the hiring cost" (Auditor General, 2011, p. 20)

After the event many of these companies disputed the description of fraud and claimed they were never finally paid for their work.

Some examples of fraud in events are:

- Misrepresenting the event in the marketing in order to stimulate ticket sales.
- Selling fake tickets to the event.
- Falsifying the event description to the Government to obtain permission, then changing the event.
- Using the event budget to purchase personal items.
- Intentionally falsifying account reports.
- Taking out cancellation insurance and covertly making sure the event does not happen.
- Match or competition fixing.
- Blagging: entering the event gates pretending to be a staff member or supplier.

False marketing can be considered fraud if it involves purposely providing misleading or deceptive information to the attendee and create financial gain. More generally, fraud entails a deliberate act of deception to obtain an unfair advantage, typically in the form of financial gain.

In the context of marketing, if the event organisation or their marketing team falsely advertises the features, benefits, or performance of the event so as to entice people to buy tickets or come to the free event, and if this misleading information influences a person's decision and results in harm to the consumer, it can be considered fraud. This is because the event marketing is misrepresenting the truth and causing financial harm to people by inducing them to purchase something based on false information.

As the term 'corruption' typically describes the abuse of power or authority for personal or private gain, often within a governmental or corporate context, false marketing may not necessarily be considered corruption on its own. It is however an unethical business practice and can involve elements of dishonesty or deception.

Preventing vendor fraud

This study focuses on a common situation with events such as public festivals and concerts around the world. It concerns the underreporting of income by vendors at an event when the agreement is to pay the event organisers a percentage of sales income. A vendor is a company or person who sells products at an event. It could be restaurants, souvenir stalls, specialist products of interest to attendees, such as car parts at a car race or works of art. A large number of vendor stalls may form a temporary market place within the event. A simple back of the envelope calculation can estimate the amount of money involved.

Vendor fraud illustrates many aspects of corruption and how petty corruption, when accumulated, can mean major financial loss to the event. The event organisers, by creating the event, have created the situation for the vendors to sell and the event has gathered the customers in the one area. For this, the organisers can charge a fixed fee to the vendors or, as is common, a percentage of the sales at the event. It may seem a minor problem, but with, for example, a 30 day festival with millions of attendees and high end restaurants, the fraud can amount to millions of dollars. In this section we survey the methods used around the world and examine the latest ideas in vendor/event relations to minimise this fraud.

Story 14: Carnet

The touring event presents many opportunities for corrupt practices. If equipment is taken to another country as part of a touring event, it can be sold for cash in the host country. No record is kept and an event becomes a method of smuggling equipment from one country to another. The equipment can also be used to conceal drugs. As pointed out by Howard Marks in his many candid interviews, he used the touring event to smuggle drugs around the world. It was so successful that he manufactured the electronic gear so it could easily conceal drugs. (Fielder, 2016). The protection against using this method of moving equipment is the *carnet*. The carnet is a list of goods that are taken out of the country. It is a passport for the goods. It is checked by Customs when the event company exits the country and when it returns. It is to make sure that all the equipment going out is brought back and there for no import duty needs to be paid.

The corrupt, being endlessly resourceful, list the goods exiting the country in a vague manner. The new equipment is sold in the foreign country and old or equipment that does not work is put in its place. The returning goods have the same name and may look the same but are inferior. It can work the other way, take out the old goods and swap them for new goods and so avoid any import duty.

Most public events have an economy on site. Goods and services are traded for money. This is possibly one of the most common areas of low level fraud. If the vendor is on a commission basis, i.e. pays the event organisation a percentage of their sales, then there is exposure. The section examines what can be done to minimise this risk.

The on-site economy

The on-site economy must be understood to be able to find the anomalies that indicate fraud. Although the amount of money that can be hidden in a local festival is small, there are a lot of local festivals around the world. Possibly the total amount of fraud is staggering. Figure 5.1 illustrates the incoming and outgoing for a public event. Just to put this in perspective. A local event, such as a concert in a park, may have 30,000 people come over a few days. If we assume each person spends only $50 then the economy is at least $1.5 million dollars. It is not uncommon for a local area, such as a small town or large suburb, to have 20 events of this nature. The economy is then $30 million dollars. The inflow and outflow of the on-site economy of a local event is illustrated in Figure 5.1. In this case the Council is the local authority. There is a large amount of financial leakage out of the area through the vendors and the suppliers.

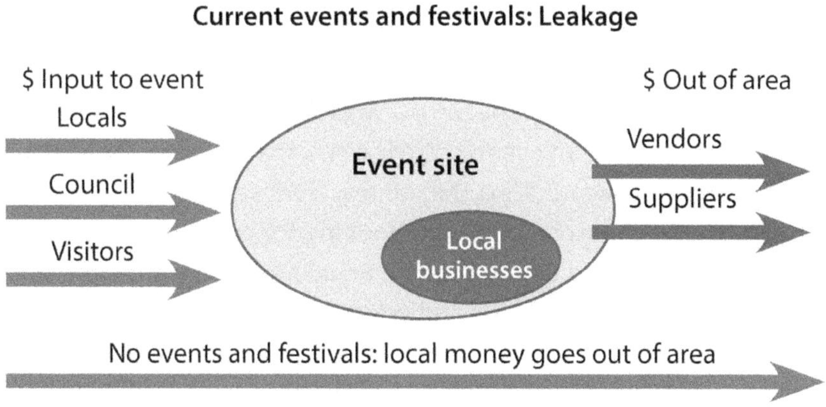

Figure 5.1: On-site economy: local event

New directors and large public events

The major issue with rationalising the event site economy is the lack of event knowledge by the directors of the new events. In many cases these can be political appointments. They assume that events and festivals are easy to organise and do not have the skills and knowledge necessary to run a high risk project. This risk is transferred to the extra money that is paid for every aspect of the event. It is the cost of ignorance. It is the same around the world, but particularly obvious in centralised economies. The foreign companies take advantage of this and flock to the country to get a piece of the pie. This forces up prices. Often there is no time to compare prices, call on expertise in event negotiation or have a bidding process for vendors. Such an event must be looked on as a test event. After a number of test events, it should be very straightforward for the event organising committee to assess the value of the event site and have a good idea of the event economy.

A note on negotiating

There are a number of factors that make events and festivals unique when compared to business and projects. The concept of an elusive attraction is one of them. The attraction must be able to attract a large audience to pay, travel and give up time. Leading up to the event, the attraction – such as a singer, boxer, team, entertainer – may be a popular one week and not the next week. So at the very heart of an event, there is a risk that is out of the control of the event managers. Next the interest from sponsors may vary dramatically. Sponsors are always looking for events for marketing. This is a highly fluid environment. For example, if an annual event does not attract the expected audience, then the vendors will not want to be involved in the next year as they won't make their money. This diminishes the quality of the event and reduces the audience numbers.

Revenue sharing/commissions

The reason for sharing the revenue with the vendors is to reduce the upfront rent cost to the vendor and therefore make the event attractive to the vendor. Part of the financial risk for the vendor is then shared with the event organisers. Once again this is used to establish a festival or event. So the up front cost is lowered, which means more or better quality vendors, which means more audience is attracted to the event and satisfied with the event, which means they come back next year. All this is fine to a point. Once the festival or event has established itself then the vendors can fully accept the risk of paying the rent up front (Figure 5.2).

First year
How to attract vendors to event
Share profit
Low initial cost for vendor
Best vendors attracted to event
Attendees enjoy quality event
Attendees recommend and come back next year
Year One event a success
Next year
Charge higher rent
and
or
Implement cashless system

Figure 5.2: Why revenue sharing or commission

Trade practices

The event site represents *restricted trade*. Often the regional and new festival organisers do not realise this and do not use it to their advantage. For example in most countries the festival can restrict the food and beverage to certain companies. This is unlike outside the site where it is illegal to restrict trade. A vendor will pay a premium to make sure their competitors are not on-site. This must be factored in to the negotiation with the vendors. As stated, new festival directors have a habit of believing they are lucky to have vendors on site. This fact is well known to the vendors.

Table 5.1 shows the various ways to estimate the on-site event economy and how to minimise the risk of vendor fraud. The solution that is gradually moving around the world is to completely control the flow of money on the event site. Not every event is comfortable with the digital control of money – i.e. a cashless system. It centralises the risk. The final method in the table of partnering illustrates the economics of trust. Partnering is also related to integrity. Here the solution is to increase the trust and integrity as a method of minimising this risk.

Table 5.1: Survey of ways to minimise vendor fraud

Description	**Issues**
Satellite account	
The city or town is regarded as a 'satellite' - an enclosed economy - with inputs and outputs and the movement of money, goods and services. All transaction are identified and checked by tracking and gaps. The gap is the economy before the event compared to the result of it.	As every industry and service transaction is tracked it is an expensive project as each sector of the economy must be covered.
Value-added Cards/Cashless	
Similar to public transport cards, these are pre-loaded with credit and used for all transactions on site. It allows complete information on all transactions. The public are becoming used to these, particularly using mobiles. 60% of festivals in USA have gone cashless. This may be approximate – but it shows the trend. With the app the 'card' can be loaded during the event.	In the past there have been fraud issues with this system. One festival used this to cover for lack of funds. People have to trust the event. The vendors may not be happy with this, which may indicate the problem vendors.

Description	Issues
VAT/GST	
If the VAT/GST system is government enforced on the transaction of all goods and services and the reporting period is every three months, the taxation department would have a good record of outliers. However the data tends to be aggregated data not specific to individual vendors. Also there are privacy issues.	As the government tax authority is behind the GST/VAT system, people are less likely to commit fraud on a large scale. Hence the vendors are very aware of keeping any 'extra' costs down. VAT/GST system compares sales across the years and any outlier is quickly spotted.
Tokens	
Once a common system in USA, attendees buy tokens from the event stall and use them to buy goods and services on site. It gives information on total vendor day transactions, but not individual ones. The vendors at the conclusion of the event exchange their tokens for money. It was primarily used for the bars on site as this was where the theft and misappropriation were the most common.	It is an old system when compare to value wallet or card on mobile. It requires staff. The token system was replaced by the cashless card in many events.
Risk and audit person	
It is common for boards to have a person or committee responsible for these types of issues. They look for risks – such as underreporting and bring it to the attention of the board. In this case they are in charge of anomaly analysis.	The person can responsible for all the risks of corruption. It is one of the recommendations in all the literature.
Observation	
People can be trained to watch vendors and their transactions. (They are called 'clickers' in malls). They observe the transaction and ask attendees what was bought. This gives a sample of the transactions and is used to extrapolate the amount changing hands over the event.	It gives a very approximate measure of the exchanges on site. It is a good start to realise just how much is spent at an event by a person or a family.
Comparison	
The vendors are expected to report daily back to the event office. From these reports the 'outliers' are discovered, i.e. those that underreport their takings. They are not invited back for next year.	None. This is often used when the organisers trust the vendors and are willing to take the risks that some will under report.

Description	Issues
Survey	
Commonly used in tourism. Attendees are asked about their spend during the event.	As with observation, this is indicative of the economy on site. Often students are used, with the skewed results. But this can be corrected in the final report.
Auction the places on site	
The vendors bid to be in the event and for the positions on site. It can be done on the web. The vendors know how much a position on site is worth. This directly relates to their takings and profit.	This is the best method of finding the correct market value of the event to the vendors and rationalising the event economy.
POS Machine	
POS machines are hired by the event office and given to the vendors for any transactions on site. The money goes to the event bank account, and vendors are paid their share at the end of each day.	Vendors have to agree.
Proxy measures and estimating	
This is used to get an overall view of the economy of the event site. For example if 100,000 people go to an event for a day, they will each spend at least $100 for food, gifts, rides, etc. Hence the economy has an input of $10million. Where does it go? Does the reporting from the vendors add up to this figure? If not then this is an indicator of leakage.	One slight drawback is estimating the number of people at an event. People come and go. However proxy measure of numbers, such as amount of waste, number of cars, even water bottles sold, will all give figures that can be combined (Kalman filter) to give a fairly accurate number.
Input/output	
The amount of raw material and goods coming onto the site is used to measure the amount sold.	This type of control is only possible in Malls where stock must be cleared on arrival.
Sponsors	
The event site only has suppliers from sponsors, e.g. Pepsi. From their records the amount of goods sold can be checked against the vendor records.	Not all goods on site will come from sponsors. However this is a good proxy measure and there would be a relationship between the sponsor's products and others sold at the event.

Description	Issues
Partnering	
Instead of just contracting the vendors, the event organisation 'partners' with the vendors. They become part of the events development. They contribute ideas to improve the events and its quality. Hence the events success is dependent on the vendors eliminating fraud.	Vendors become stakeholders, not just in the money, but in the long term success of the event. Major vendors such as restaurants then have a long term contract with the event. The issue is inertia of the event and the monopoly by long term vendors.

Partnering is an example of the theme of this textbook. It is about trust and integrity. Of course this is not possible with every vendor or every event, however it is the direction to take to minimise the fraud. When everyone shares the success, everyone contributes and this helps to keep others on track. In which case, the vendors themselves are the ears and the eyes of the vigilance that is needed to mitigate this risk.

Steve Schmader, CFEE, and the President & CEO of the International Festivals & Events Association, ran a highly successful citywide festival for many years (before the detailed tracking apps available today existed). His event, the Boise River Festival in Idaho, had up to 200 vendors. Steve, in a personal interview, said that he trusted his vendors. If or when there looked like an issue of under-reporting may be occurring, the vendor simply wouldn't be invited back the next year, given that their sales numbers were not keeping pace with the other vendors. This was a simple and effective method based on trust, quality, and making the vendors part of the event experience.

Ticket fraud

Ticketing is a prime area for corruption. Fraud seems the most common form of corruption in ticketing for events. It is so common that it has its own terminology.

Ticket fraud can include:

- Misleading information about the event including ticket speculation.

- Fake tickets.
- Fake websites: pretending to be the event website selling the tickets.
- Drip pricing.

Story 15: Ticket reseller

The court found that the company, a ticket reseller, made false or misleading representations to consumers. The company claimed it was the official seller of tickets to particular events and that the tickets were scarce. Also that the price shown on the site was much cheaper than the consumer would actually have to pay. The real fee was not disclosed until late into the booking process. The company was ordered to pay a penalty of $7 million. (ACCC, 2020).

Ticket speculation is selling tickets online using fraudulent information and deceptive websites. The line between describing the benefits and exaggerating the benefits is not a clear one. Particularly for many people when they are promoting an event and their profit or contract depends on the number of tickets sold. It can be a mistake of marketing or an intentional lie. Pretending that the tickets are 'almost all sold out' to give a sense of urgency to the sale is very common, but is fraudulent if it is not true. In the author's experience, there is almost a 'gung ho' attitude to this kind of fraud in the events sector.

The tickets on sale may be advertised as VIP or special but when the patron arrives at the event they find it is a general admission ticket. In the truly fraudulent, they may not have the tickets to sell at all and they send fake tickets or nothing at all. This includes selling exhibition space online without actually owning it. As the sale does not come from the actual event, there are no refunds if the event is cancelled or the patron turns up to find the ticket is fake.

Story 16: Champions League

A well reported case of ticketing fraud was the investigation into the violence, robbery and mayhem outside the Champions League in Paris in 2022. Although the intention was to have complete digital ticketing, the UK Liverpool Club decided to allocate 20,000 paper tickets. The 2023 report prepared by the Union of European Football Associations (UEFA) describes and analyses the ticket fraud at the request of the French Government. Printed ticket did not include 'enhanced traceability procedure', such as swapping the receipt with their name on it as proof or purchase for a coloured wrist band at the security entrance.

The scams included:

- Tickets with fraudulently created barcodes.
- Direct copies of existing tickets. One ticket was copied over 700 times.
- Blagging: Some bought fake tickets cheaply knowing they could enter the Stade de France but not the perimeter. They would then find a way to enter the event – jump the turnstiles, tailgate others through the turnstiles or just force their way past the officials.

Blagging was quite new to the report as the previous fake ticket scams for finals were mainly directed at the buyer. In this case the buyer knew full well about the fake tickets. In the words of the report *"However, this was the first time that fraud was observed in such proportions."*

At three of the gates, one in ten tickets was a fake ticket. The result was delays, overcrowding at the gates and closing of some entrances. (UCLF22, 2023)

The final word on ticketing has to go to the Auditor General's report on the Commonwealth Games. It demonstrates the way corruption and incompetence are too often intertwined:

> *" This dismal performance (15% of expected sales) was attributable to a critically delayed appointment of the ticketing consultant and the ticketing agency, inadequate marketing, low ticket sales and spectator attendance, and excessive distribution of complimentary tickets (especially high value tickets), paradoxically coupled with reports of non-availability of tickets."* (Auditor General, 2011, p. 136).

Drip pricing is a practice where a price is advertised at the beginning of an online purchase, but then extra fees and charges, such as booking and service fees, are gradually added during the purchase process. This can result in consumers paying far more than they initially intended to.

The fraudster will actively scan websites and social media to look for people desperate to buy a ticket. The sense of urgency is an important factor in a successful fraud. This form of scamming is described extensively in publications and websites for banks. There are three characteristics:

- **Authority**: the scammer appears to have power, exclusivity or a special arrangement. Such as a special access to event tickets.
- **Urgency**: this is to confuse and not allow time to check up or compare.
- **Action**: the scam must have a call for an action.

It is interesting to read the experience of people who have been scammed into attending predatory conferences (Story 17). It is surprisingly similar to the Fyre Festival. Some of the descriptions include: Welcome party that took only 30 minutes, food was cheap lunch box and tea, small crowded rooms, presentations with no research and just photos of a destination.

One example of the extent of the predatory conference scam, the US Federal Trade Commission took legal action against OMICS, iMedPub, and Conference Series.

Story 17: Predatory Conference

An interesting and highly specialised scam is the predatory conference. This is outgrowth of the modern academic need to publish. An academic's career is dependent on measures related to publishing and citations. The impersonal algorithmic rating system over the web has further enabled the fraud. A predatory conference is one that exists but has no international academic standing. To quote the American librarian, Jeffrey Beall, who has explored this scam in detail:

"These are not conferences organized by scholarly societies. Instead, they are conferences organized by revenue-seeking companies that want to exploit researchers' need to build their vitas with conference presentations and papers in the published proceedings or affiliated journals" (Beall, 2015, p. 2).

The characteristics of the predatory conferences can be used to spot other event scams. The key, as ever, is the money. The academics pay a registration fee for the conference and pay for their paper to be placed in a bogus online journal. This is similar to other event fraud. The characteristics include:

- ☐ An email address as the only channel of communication
- ☐ The website has no legal information such as company registration number and claims to be non- profit.
- ☐ There is advertised an award system for the presentations and the papers, e g. Best paper
- ☐ Often the conference will advertise key speakers who do not turn up and know nothing about the conference.
- ☐ The time for presentation at the conference is short so it can attract as many academics as possible.
- ☐ The name of the conference is broad to include as many registrations as possible.
- ☐ The conference occurs is a country with lax anti-fraud laws.
- ☐ The turn around time for approval of a submitted paper is quick. Indicating the lack of any review process.
- ☐ Some of the submitted papers are absurd.

They were fined $50.1 million for engaging in deceptive business practices. Below is a quote from the proceedings:

> *In order to attract consumers, Defendants advertise the attendance and participation of prominent academics and researchers.... The FTC has provided evidence, however, that Defendants advertise the attendance and participation of these individuals without their permission or actual affiliation... In numerous instances, individuals have requested unsuccessfully to have their names removed from Defendants' conference advertising materials. ... In some instances, Defendants did not remove an individuals' name until the threat of legal action.* (United Sates District Court, Nevada, 2019. p. 10)

Once again we recognise the similarity with other event scams such as the fake attraction: the rap artist, the academic stars or the influencers. As well as the list above there are other red flags that a conference may be fraudulent. Surveying the comments on these conferences gives us a few extra indicators such as:

1. Email requests from the attendee asking for more information to the conference that are either never answered or vaguely worded.
2. Contacts for the event seem to be away travelling or unavailable.
3. The website is unprofessional and overly optimistic.
4. Spelling and grammar mistakes.
5. When the advertised speakers are contacted, they have no knowledge of the conference.
6. It seems too good to be true, such as cheap registration for the level of the event and preferential hotel rates.
7. Leveraging the registration with immediate insistent appeals to attend other events.
8. Emails lack a reply address.
9. The organising company or person has a vague address such as just the name of the state e.g. Nevada.
10. Emails have a click throughs that seems strange.

Exercise

Explore the similarities of the Fyre Festival and the Predatory Conferences. The excellent work of Jeffrey Beal is found online.

Advanced questions

- How did the courts decide on a figure of $50 million.
- What was their criteria?
- Does OMIC and co still organise conferences?
- Research the fake film festivals. To have a film judged and shown at the festival the filmmaker pays a submission fee. Note that the red flags indicating a fake film festival are similar to those indicating a predatory conference.

Story 18: Dodgy detecting

A new form of event is the metal detecting event, often billed as a treasure hunt. It is now found around the world and includes camping, vendors, prizes and sponsors. The aim is to find interesting and or valuable objects using a metal detector. A form of laundering was rumoured. The dishonest person illegally scans a heritage site when there is no one there, such as a night. If they find an object, it would be impossible to sell as it was illegally found. The person then goes to a metal detecting event, and 'finds' the object at the event. This gives it a legal provenance. The object has been laundered, or cleaned of its real origin. Also there are suspicions that some dishonest owners of the event secretly place interesting objects on a site so it can be found. This make the event look good in comparison to similar events and attracts more people.

Exercise

- ☐ Research ticket fraud on the web. There are many sites.
- ☐ Compile a list of do's and don'ts when buying tickets.

Collusion

To collude means to secretly cooperate or conspire with others, typically for illegal or deceitful purposes. It often implies a level of dishonesty or manipulation, where individuals or groups work together to achieve a common goal that is unethical or harmful to others.

The European Commission gives a wide, yet succinct, definition of collusion:

> *"The term collusion in public procurement (often also referred to as "bid-rigging") refers to illegal agreements between economic operators, with the aim of distorting competition in award procedures. Such agreements between economic operators to collude may assume various forms, such as fixing the content of their tenders beforehand (especially the price) in order to influence the outcome of the procedure, refraining from submitting a tender, allocating the market based on geography, contracting authority or the subject of the procurement or setting up rotation schemes for a number of procedures. The aim of all these practices is to enable a predetermined tenderer to secure a contract while creating the impression that the procedure is genuinely competitive."* (European Commission, 2021, p. 4).

The immediate, and ultimate, results of collusive practices are:

- Undermines integrity and therefore trust in all agreements undertaken for the event.
- Prevents innovation, response to changes and therefore the development of the events.
- Halts new upcoming companies from entering the market.
- Significantly increases cost and diminishes the quality of the services or products.
- Often in tandem with other forms of corruption such as bribery and extortion.
- Leads to civil and criminal legal prosecution and loss of event reputation.

In the long term it creates inertia in, what should be, a dynamic responsive events sector. As a result, mega events are favoured, eventually become entrenched and stale needing more and more support from the public purse.

Based on worldwide anecdotal evidence of event professionals this is a well known risk in the industry when dealing with suppliers. For example, suppliers making prior arrangements in what appears to be free competition. This is a procurement risk that can reduce the quality and increase the cost of the goods and services. As with all elements of corruption, it can also open the door to extortion, bribery and fraud. Collusion in procurement for projects, such as private public partnerships, is so common around the world and involves such large amounts of money, particularly with development projects, that the information is readily available.

Story 19: Sumo stats

Match fixing by competitors is an example of collusion. The Japan Sumo Association (JSA) cancelled a grand tournament as a result of investigation of match fixing by the Sumo wrestlers. This is an example of the identification of corruption through the use of mathematics and pattern recognition. The nature of sport with its competitive hierarchy, winners going on to the next level, meant that the data was easily analysed. With other events this is impossible unless they are repeat events. The book *Freakonomics: A rogue economist explores the hidden side of everything* (Levitt, 2005), illustrates how the use of statistics over time uncovered the issue with match fixing and Sumo wrestling. It is worth noting that two of the Sumo wrestlers who were about to expose the corruption died of the same cause in the same hospital only hours apart without an autopsy. This serves as a reminder of how deeply corruption can infect a system, its secrecy and reach.

Other types of collusion in events include anything which involves competitions such as: guessing competitions, beauty contests, music and film awards. Perhaps the most interesting collusion that was exposed and studied in detail occurred in the Sumo wrestling events in Japan. In this case mathematical analysis uncovered patterns of match fixing.

The practice is so widespread in project based industries that there are sub classification. All of these are known in the event sector. In the *2024 Guide to Combating Corruption & Fraud in Development Project*, the International Anti-Corruption Resource Center describes these subdivisions:

- **Complementary bidding or shadow bids**: The suppliers of the one resource or service get together and arrange that only one will put in a quote that is realistic. The other suppliers inflate their price or give a defective quote. This arrangement ensures the one supplier gets the job. The winning supplier pays the other suppliers with kickback or favours. The negative side for the event is they may not be the best and the price is inflated. It is almost impossible to stop for a single event.
- **Bid rotation**: The supplier has an agreement with the other suppliers that they will divide up the events and not quote against each other. In this way they can share the events according to time or geography.
- **Bid suppression**: The collusive group ensure that other suppliers do not get a chance to quote. This can be accomplished by threats or bribing the relevant member of the event team to ignore the other quotes.

(International Anti-Corruption Resource Center, 2024).

Their excellent website and document has a section called *Red Flags of Collusive Bidding.* This is directed at major projects with large budgets and continuous work. For the events the red flags that indicate collusion are not as obvious. However it can be distilled from this list. One that the author has come across is when the winning quote then hires the other companies as subcontractors. This would be part collusive deal between suppliers. In some countries, subcontracting the work is very common. So much so that the subcontractor then contracts it further down the line. The result is a significant loss of quality and increase in risk.

For events, these red flags include:

- Small common mistakes in the various tender documents indicate they may be written by the one company.
- Some of the tender documents are so below standard that they are expected to be rejected.
- The price does not make sense. Some are just too high when compared to industry standards.

For example a local authority advertises a new festival and asks for equipment suppliers, such as sound, fencing, stages to contact them with an 'expression of interest' in being part of the event. The local authority cuts this down to three suppliers, A,B and C, assuming they will get a fair and honest proposal from these. However unbeknown to the authority, the suppliers have made a compact to ensure only one will get the job. The others over price their bid. The suppliers had made a deal amongst themselves that they share future events and help each other.

Price fixing is another form of collusion in the event sector. It is setting the price of a product rather than allowing it to be determined by free-market forces. Fixing a price is illegal in many countries if it involves collusion among producers or suppliers. Even an association of suppliers can stray into this area if they have 'recommended' prices. This again is the border zone.

Discovering and combatting collusive bidding is a major reason for an event organisation to be a member of the professional organisation such as the International Festivals & Event Association (IFEA), International Live Events Association (ILEA), Meeting Professionals International or a local one such as the New Zealand Events Association (NZEA).

Collusive practices can be stopped by ensuring the suppliers are partners in the event. They share the profits, the goodwill and also the risk if other suppliers collude to force up prices. They are also the ears and eyes of the event. This is a solution that is part of economics of trust described in Chapter 3 and the culture of integrity in Chapter 10.

Event companies are also subject to this risk. Event companies colluding in the bid to manage a public or government event can be subject to fines, civil and even criminal action. It comes under competition and antitrust laws in many countries.

It also can be the collusion of judges of a competition, such as a film festivals and beauty pageants to rig the results. It occurs when the criteria for a competition is intangible or not directly measureable. The results of these have such important financial implications that collusion is a common accusation. With regard to a film festival, it can involve producers, directors, actors, buyers, sales agents, distributers all trying to influence the judges.

Bias is not the same as collusion or conflict of interest. In a competition that involves, for example, performance, beauty or art, unless it is a simple measure, the judges will have bias. The judges have a background in the field, their individual experience and theories. Although there may be criteria involved, it is inevitable their decisions will be subjective. If the bias is understood, it can be taken into account in the decisions. This border zone of subjectivity and criteria is where people will try to influence the judges. A mitigating factor on this type of influence is the reputation of the judges. The judges want to be, and appear, fair. (Bouwens et al., 2022).

Summary

- ☐ Definition of fraud
- ☐ Examples of fraud
- ☐ Intangible nature of events
- ☐ Exaggerated marketing, the border zone and the descent into fraud
- ☐ Story: Non-existent event, camel beauty
- ☐ Vendor fraud and partnering
- ☐ Ticket speculation
- ☐ Drip pricing
- ☐ Story: Ticket reseller, Champions League, Dodgy Detecting
- ☐ Collusion: definition
- ☐ Negative results
- ☐ Types of collusion
- ☐ Story: Sumo Stats
- ☐ Bias

References

ACCC. (2020). Viagogo to pay $7 million for misleading consumers. www.accc.gov.au/media-release/viagogo-to-pay-7-million-for-misleading-consumers

Auditor General. (2011). *Audit Report 2010 Commonwealth Games in India,* Comptroller and Auditor General of India, Union Government (Civil) Report No 6 of 2011-12. https://cag.gov.in/en/audit-report/details/2586

Beall, J. (2015). Another Taiwan-based mega-scholarly conference organizer emerges. *Scholarly Open Access*. https://scholarlyo.com/another-taiwan-based-mega-scholarly-conference-organizer-emerges/

Bouwens, J., Hofmann, C. & Lechner, C. (2022). *Transparency and Biases in Subjective Performance Evaluation*. TRR 266 Accounting for

Transparency Working Paper Series No. 72. https://papers.ssrn.com/sol3/papers.cfm?abstract_id=4012905

European Commission. (2021). *Final Notice on tools to fight collusion.* 15.3.2021 C(2021) 1631. https://op.europa.eu/en/publication-detail/-/publication/6a2458e1-878c-11eb-ac4c-01aa75ed71a1/language-en

International Anti-Corruption Resource Center. (2024). Guide to Combating Corruption & Fraud in Development Projects, https://guide.iacrc.org/

Office of the City Auditor. (2021). *Fraud Risk Management Policy.* Gainesville Florida. www.gainesvillefl.gov/files/assets/public/v/1/city-auditor/documents/2021-10-fraud-risk-management-policy.pdf

Silverstone, H., Sheetz, M., Pedneault, S. and Rudewicz, F. (2012). *Forensic Accounting and Fraud Investigation for Non-Experts 3rd Ed.*, NY: John Wiley & Sons.

Transparency International. (2009). *The Anti-Corruption Plain Language Guide.* https://ciaotest.cc.columbia.edu/wps/ti/0018979/f_0018979_16239.pdf

UEFA Champions League Final Independent Review Panel. (2022). *UCLF22 independent review: Appendix.* https://editorial.uefa.com/resources/0282-1899c8c4c7a4-e0d6a874ad67-1000/uclf22_independent_review_appendix.pdf

United Sates District Court, Nevada. (2019). *Case 2:16-cv-02022-GMN-VCF* https://www.ftc.gov/system/files/documents/cases/de_121_-_omics_order_granting_summary_judgment.pdf

6 Conflict of Interest

The following sections concern the groups of types of corruption: conflict of interest, extortion, nepotism, favouritism, money laundering and privacy/data breaches. They are often interrelated and interwoven with fraud and bribery. It is easier to steal from a thief than an honest man as the thief will never report it. Unfortunately this can imply the den of thieves who will never hire an honest person.

Mark Twain:

> *"To steal from a thief is not theft but merely larceny from a dishonest man."*

Louis L'Amour's book *The Walking Drum* states:

> *"Lie to a liar, for lies are his coin; steal from a thief, for that is easy; lay a trap for a trickster and catch him at the first attempt, but beware of an honest man"* .

A conflict of interest in an organization occurs when an individual or entity has competing interests or loyalties that could potentially bias their decision-making or actions, to the detriment of the organization's best interests. With events it is almost impossible for some of the staff not to have a conflict of interest. It may not be to the detriment of the organisation's best interest. In fact a well-networked member of the staff who is active in the event industry is often a huge benefit to finding the right suppliers and dealing with the stakeholders, such as the sponsors.

In other words a conflict of interest is not corruption on its own but can pose the risk of corruption. This means that if it is not dealt with, the consequences can be legal prosecution and loss of reputation. If a member of the event team has private interests different and possibly competing with the interest of the event, then their ability to act in the best interest of the event can be impaired.

Examples of a conflict of interest in the events sector are:

- A member of the event organising group takes business opportunities for themselves when it was offered to the team or company.
- Awarding supplier contracts to companies of relatives.
- Using insider information only privy to the event team to buy securities for personal benefit.
- Using owned or hired assets of the event for private advantage.
- Part-owning a company that is bidding for a contract with the event.

According to the *2023 Handbook of Good Practices in the Fight Against Corruption*, most conflict of interest occurs in the awarding of contracts, bidding and tendering and in the recruitment, hiring and promotion of staff. (European Commission, 2023). This first part certainly applies to the mega events as they are similar to the public–private partnerships in infrastructure development. For many years the Olympics, for example, entailed massive construction and infrastructure change, such as roads, rail, brown field developments, accommodation and much more. These introduced opportunities for corruption on a huge scale involving all levels of government and business.

A form of conflict of interest, pointed out by Graycar and Prenzler in *Understanding and Preventing Corruption,* is called self dealing (2013). It is an individual taking advantage of their position in an organisation to increase their personal benefit outside of the responsibilities to the company. This looks at the favouritism from the perpetrator's point of view.

The OECD definition of conflict of interest (COI) is *"when a public official has private-capacity interests which could improperly influence the performance of their official duties and responsibilities."* (OECD, 2020, p. 222). This can easily be expanded to include people in companies and organisations themselves. An example in the events sector would be a festival manager holding shares in a company that is competing for work at a public event. This may not be an issue if the conflict of interest is declared.

It is almost inevitable that an experienced event company will have multiple relationships with many supplier companies. A government event office will be dealing with a multitude of events. In some cases they are just the host of the event, which means they make decisions to allow the event to proceed, or they may be bidding for an event. They may also be funding and assisting with the management functions, marketing for example. They may have, as part of their event portfolio, the responsibility to create and completely manage events. In all these cases the event office will be working with multiple suppliers, sound, catering, staging and many more. It can be complex, fluid and dynamic. The events industry is very personable and it is highly likely that people will know each other. These informal networks may assist finding and managing the right suppliers. Keeping track of any personal or professional conflict of interest may well be impossible. Hence this must be set up as a clear part of the governance of the event and become accepted practice of the staff to self exclude if there is an issue. Once again it illustrates the importance of trust in an events organisation.

Adapting the International Chamber of Commerce, Guidelines on Conflicts of Interest in Enterprises (ICC, 2018) and the Overview of Anti-Corruption Compliance Standards and Guidelines (Ivanov, 2022), when facing a conflict of interest in event management, the following actions can be taken:

- **Avoidance**: A conflict of interest or potential conflict of interest could be avoided by relinquishing certain roles or connections. For example: a music festival organizer stepping down from their position on the board of a competing festival, or a conference planner selling their shares in a venue they frequently book for events. The event management team may restrict the availability of information and the responsibility of the individual if they believe there is a conflict.

- **Disclosure**: If all parties are informed of a conflict of interest, the relationship may proceed. For instance a concert promoter disclosing that their spouse's band is being considered for inclusion in the event program, or an exhibition curator revealing that their sibling is one of the artists being showcased, or a festival organiser making known to the board of the festival their long term friendship with the head of the security company employed by the event.
- **Stepping back**: It may be appropriate for someone with a conflict of interest to recuse themselves from certain decisions. For example: a festival food vendor coordinator abstaining from the selection process when they have shares in various restaurant companies that may benefit or a conference speaker selection committee member removing themselves from discussions about a close colleague's submission.
- **Refusal**: Rejecting the circumstance creating a conflict of interest can eliminate the issue entirely. This could involve an art exhibition judge declining a gift from a participating artist or a music festival organizer refusing a free vacation offered by a potential sponsor.

To mitigate this risk there are a number of solutions. The conflict of interest issue should be clearly defined for all the staff and volunteers. This can be backed up by having these issues discussed during training sessions or in risk management meetings. It should be part of the policy and the code of conduct for the event. The leadership should set an example to the rest of the team in declaring any conflict of interest. These solutions are found in the Chapter 8 on Prevention and 10 on Governance.

During the event planning and implementation phase, the organisers should create a register of interests and a system for the active management of the issues, such as exclusion from decisions and resigning from the position.

Conflict of interest may require an independent third party to assess the situation. Outright rejection of an employee or volunteer because of a perceived conflict of interest may be seen as bias.

Story 20: Board malfeasance

Not all corruption is straightforward. One very successful event with over $5 million in ticket sales per annum, was overseen by an event board. The event team reported to the Board and this type of legal structure was required by the local authority. The Board comprise of 12 people. To be a member of the Board required a majority vote of the Board. One of the more astute members of the Board noticed a gradual change in its composition. At the same time the Board seemed to be devaluing the event. Suppliers were being overpaid. These actions were not helping the event grow and the numbers of attendees were dwindling. At this stage the more astute member realised that certain people had been voted onto the Board to secretly collapse the event. The event would then be privatised and bought at a bargain price by friends of the new Board members. Once it passed into private hands, the event would be reinvigorated. This is against the rules of public boards, but was done gradually so there was no real proof.

Extortion

Extortion is the purposeful demand of an action, goods or money using the threat of violence or exposure of illegal activity. Extortion is one of the possible consequences of bribery and other corrupt practices. It is one reason corrupt practices are tradeable. The act of bribing an official can be used to extort more money from the person giving the bribe and the official accepting the bribe.

In the event business extortion can include threatening to expose a sponsor or the event team to adverse publicity in exchange for favours , such as tickets, money or services. Once again the deadline is the issue. The extortionist can, for example threaten to create negative publicity over the internet and social media. The event team will not have enough time or social reach to negate the effect.

Extortion is well hidden as indicated by the cyber extortion of companies and universities. The full extent of this is unknown, but there are indicators of many major payoffs. There are movements around the world by governments to make the reporting of cyber-extortion a legal requirement of a company. This is a good indicator of the importance of this hidden practice. The cost of the loss of reputation is more than the cost of paying the extortionist. It is worth noting that this type of corruption, i.e. extortion using the cyber world, creates a risk to almost every event around the world.

Extortion is the tool of the gangs. Standover and threats can come from any organised group, even the police in some countries. The reports around the world include the drug cartels in Mexico demanding percentages from vendors at events. The crime of extortion, in some jurisdictions, can result in a sentence of up to 20 years in jail and a fine of a quarter of a million dollars.

The colloquial use of the term extortion may also refer to the actions of an organisation in raising the price of a good or service when the customer is trapped and has no choice. The organisation is maximising profit by taking advantage of people in difficulty, such as charging exorbitant rent when a festival is nearby or tripling the fares when the audience is leaving and taxis are scarce. Is this extortion or normal business practice? The participants may see it as extortion. This is in the border zone and may be normal business practice, no matter how unpleasant.

Due to the threatening aspect of extortion, evidence of it at events is difficult to find. And, as people involved may not want it public, it may be charged under a different crime and may be settled privately. Anecdotally there are plenty of stories and social media certainly has these from the event attendees, such as the Baltimore security extortion referred to in Story 21. The line between robbery with menace and extortion is not clear. The former has an immediate threat of violence. Extortion tends to involve future threats that may be physical violence, reputation damage and revealing secrets. Extortion requests can be continuous.

Story 21: Demanding money

An example of petty extortion happened at one music event in Baltimore, USA. The patrons complained of the on-site security guards demanding money, $20 or $50, or they would be escorted out of the festival.

An example of extortion: According to the USA Department of Justice in 2021 a music production company applied to hold events in a city plaza. They needed permits from the city. The production company had already contracted and hired the employees needed for the event. Three days before the event two senior employees (the defendants in this case) of the city demanded that the company hire union labour.

"Today's convictions affirm the U.S. Department of Labor Office of Inspector General's commitment to protecting the American workers from extortion and unlawful influence. The defendants used threats of financial harm to obtain wages from a television production company for services that were not needed or required. We will continue working with our law enforcement partners to combat this type of criminal activity," said Michael C. Mikulka, Special Agent-in-Charge, New York Region, U.S. Department of Labor Office of Inspector General.

(DOJ, 2019).

The concert in Story 27 *Gangsta Extortion,* is an example of petty extortion using the element of time in events. Last minute demands are very common in the events.

The manual *Resisting Extortion and Solicitation in International Transactions: A company tool for employee training,* gives a valuable and detailed list of actions. These can be adapted to the events sector and include:

Reducing the likelihood of extortion:

- Ensure there is a publicly available event policy and code of conduct.
- Provide training to event team.
- Have a known reporting mechanism.
- Include anti-corruption clauses within contracts with suppliers and others.
- Important meetings have at least two members of the event staff, with (formal or informal) minutes taken.
- Clear policy regarding gifts and hospitality.

Reducing consequence if it occurs:

- If demands are made take your time to decide and respond in writing.
- Record the incident and consider corrective action.
- Have an incentive for staff and volunteers to report demands.
- Make sure employees and volunteers know that they should not refuse payment if there is the threat of violence.

(Fox, 2011)

The whole document is comprehensive and concerns deals in foreign countries. In the experience of the author, this is well worth the event company reviewing the whole document, *RESIST Resisting Extortion and Solicitation in International Transactions, A company tool for employee training,* if they are touring events to other countries.

Favouritism, nepotism, cronyism

Favouritism, nepotism, cronyism, or clientelism is giving preferential treatment to a person at the expense of others. Favouritism is the more general term. Nepotism concerns family members and cronyism is preferential treatment to friends.

If the event company is a private company there is nothing directly illegal in the owner hiring friends or family members. In some cases the ability to work together and informal communication may be advantageous. However people within the organisation must make it clear if this is happening. It may violate specific contract agreements. Also there may be an effect on staff morale, particularly if that person is less qualified. It can reduce the integrity of the company and the trust within the team and, as has been pointed out, this is one of the pathways to other corruption.

Here are some examples:

- Employees are married to each other, or to a colleague's sibling, child or parent.
- A senior staff member's child or other close family member is given accelerated career progress. Other staff are silently fuming, seeing this as gross favouritism and a misuse of power.
- Decisions about appointments and promotions are being made on the basis of who the candidate is related to, rather than their skills and experience.
- The 'favoured' family member becomes isolated and defensive as the disapproval of colleagues and staff seeps slowly in. Alternatively, the favoured family member feels so 'at home', they make over-exuberant use of their power.
- The workplace is split into 'camps': those who support the family regime, thinking that the existence of family networks illustrates a 'family-friendly' workplace; and those who are outraged by a sense of injustice.

- There is a widespread perception that there is no point making a complaint about the favoured family member because they are part of a "protected species."

As pointed out by Public Safety Canada when quoting the Organisation for Economic Co-operation and Development (OECD) handbook on Public Integrity,

> *"Merit-based recruitment involves hiring professionals based on their qualifications (talent, skills, experience, competence) and ability to successfully complete the job rather than based on patronage or nepotism. It is believed that hiring professionals based on merit provides the necessary foundations to develop a culture of integrity, which ultimately helps to prevent corruption"* (Sauve et al. 2023, p. 23)

One cannot ignore that the nature of event planning and the compressed timeline means many event teams will hire friends and relatives. This is quite common as the informal and human aspects of events are important. The ability to work together and a common culture are part of it. This must of course be balanced against the legality of doing it, the possible lack of expertise in a specific area, the formation of powerful sub-groups within the over-all team and the ultimate cost. A group of friends may volunteer for a local festival. They are far better at their job when they are with their friends. Event planning and the event itself is not a 9 to 5 job and the informal networks, after work get-togethers and common experiences all make the individuals better at dealing with the stress and timelines of event management. Many of these aspects cannot be caught and measured in a table of employment criteria.

The advantages of having a group of people who get on well together and efficiently accomplish tasks must be weighed against the group forming a small power unit within the event. This is a problem for repeat events such as a yearly festival or conference. A cohesive group can move the event in the direction they want. In the words of one event director "they deplete the asset". They can become an inertia, refusing to change and develop the event. This is well known in events that rely on community volunteers.

As pointed out by Dr Adam Masters when examining corruption in sport:

> *"Nepotism as a form of corruption does not neatly fit into the sporting arena. A child, nephew or niece of a sporting great may also perform well due to familial socialisation, access to additional coaching and attention from their successful relatives and family associates."* (Masters, 2015, p. 115)

Patronage can also lead to favouritism and the corruption of a merit based system. The patron can be a sponsor, a politician or a philanthropist. They can push their own person into a position over the more qualified and will influence the event. As Graycar and Prenzler explain:

> *"The person so promoted becomes obligated to the patron who, in turn, may wish to seek influence, wealth, status or power. By circumventing the normal merit processes a patron can corruptly distort a transparent process and diminish integrity in decision making. Patronage in the arts is a long-standing activity, and central to the way the arts have always flourished. Patronage in politics is tied up with genuine electoral interests, and leaders elected democratically are entitled to have in their teams people of similar ideological and other values. What is important here is that the boundaries are clear and that there is transparency in processes. Patronage is the glue that holds many tribal societies together.."* (Graycar and Prenzler, 2013, p. 8)

The last sentence alludes to the feudal and tribal societies. Patronage may not be regarded as wrong and therefore not regarded as corruption in those societies. In societies where the modernisation is recent, the two systems will often, awkwardly, sit side by side. An example is a hereditary monarchy where the basis of the governance is the extended family. The family members are appointed the heads of major companies, government departments and regions. This can be quite a shock for touring event companies and events from western democracies.

Another form of corruption has the legal term 'undue influence'. It is when a person or group uses legal means to influence a decision. The gift giving and other hospitality are examples of this if the aim is to influence a decision. For example the event team may use the VIP tickets to the event as a way to influence politician's decisions about expanding the event.

Money laundering

Money laundering is the act of legitimizing illegally obtained funds by passing them through various transactions to conceal their origin. The money is thereby 'washed' or 'cleaned' of its source. This criminal practice is frequently linked to organized crime, drug trafficking, and terrorism. Once again we meet the netherworld, as textbook *Forensic Accounting and Fraud Investigation* points out :

> *"Because money laundering by its nature is a crime of concealment, the scope of money-laundering activity is not precisely known."* (Silverstone et al., 2012. p. 102)

Large amounts of money can be moved over a short period of time with many events, hence they are attractive for criminals to launder money. An event such as a big concert with entry fees can be used to change the source of the money. It appears that the money has come from ticket sales when in fact many people were allowed free entry. Over-paying an artist is another way to launder the money. This payment is an expense and can be claimed against the income. Over-invoicing is another example – it looks as though the money has gone to suppliers.

Money laundering may be uncovered by the relatively new science of forensic accounting using artificial intelligence. This involves sophisticated accounting methods that examine the economic history of the organisation to discover any discrepancies. The AI aspect, at this stage speeds up the whole discovery process and learns from every interaction.

There are three stages in laundering money: placement, layering and integration.

- **Placement** is moving and distributing the illegal money into the general financial system. Story 22 uses the technique called *smurfing*. But it can include false invoices, adding the cash to payments or moving small amounts in cash overseas. All of these have been found in the events sector.
- **Layering** concerns passing the illegally obtained funds through a number of transactions so that the origin of the money is difficult to trace.
- **Integration** is the last stage of layering where the funds are now part of the legitimate financial system and can be used for purchases.

The types of events that are most vulnerable to money laundering are ones where large amounts of money change hands and there is price flexibility. Arts events are a good example. Two other factors help this are: anonymity and cash sales. Works of art can be bought anonymously at an exhibition or art fair using corrupt money and sold later for clean cash. As pointed out in Money Laundering and Terrorist Financing in the Art and Antiquities Market:

> *"The market for cultural objects has a history of privacy and discretion."* (FATF, 2023. p. 11)

One may assume that as money laundering involves organised crime and large amounts of money that smaller events are not the target. However as is pointed out a number of times in this book, the one event may not have the sums, but a group of events can be well worth while. Smaller events can be the focus of 'structuring', another word for smurfing. Structuring involves splitting up the large amount of illegal cash into smaller amounts that can deposited in multiple bank accounts without arousing suspicion of the authorities. It makes detection of this almost impossible. The complexity of multiple smaller events is an attraction to money laundering.

Story 22: Mules

According to the Fraud for the Banking and Payments Federation Ireland (BPFI), young people are recruited at music festivals in Ireland to act as 'mules'. A mule is a person who places money into their account and then transfers it to another account thereby 'washing' the money. The amounts in each transaction are small enough not to be noticed. It is below the currency transaction reporting (CTR) requirements. The mule is often an innocent person with no idea of the larger scheme or its illegality. They are paid a fee and given all kinds of excuses for the transfer. Foreign attendees at the festivals are particularly attractive to the criminals as they have accounts overseas which makes it difficult to create an audit trail and trace the source of the money.

According to FraudSMART there were over 2,600 mule accounts identified in the first half of 2023 alone. A majority of money mule bank accounts belonged to those aged between 18 and 24 years of age. Average amount moved through accounts in the region of €10K making a total of €17.5m illegally transferred. Although this is not all from music festivals, the festivals are seen as an excellent recruiting ground for the mules. (Fraudsmart, 2024)

Exercise

Create a causal diagram (see Chapter 9) for a music festival with the final risk: money laundering via mules. Use the causes, factors, evidence, mitigating actions and Figure 9.1 Process of creating a causal analysis diagram, to work through this risk.

What other aspects of the music festival could be used for money laundering? Hint: false invoicing, ghost ticket sales, overpayment of suppliers with kickbacks.

The 2021 United States Strategy on Countering Corruption makes this observation:

> *"The markets for art and antiquities—and the market participants who facilitate transactions—are especially vulnerable to a*

range of financial crimes. Built-in opacity, lack of stable and predictable pricing, and inherent cross-border transportability of goods sold, make the market optimal for illicit value transfer, sanctions evasion, and corruption." (The Whitehouse, 2021, p.24)

Privacy/data breaches

A music concert, for example, has value in its data of the attendees. The ticket sales data contain the names and contact details of people interested in that artist or type of music. This can then be on-sold to other promoters or booking artists to enable them to target their potential market. It saves a lot of time and money and is illegal according to the privacy acts in most countries. The concert acts as a filter for the right demographic. As with all corruption this is hidden and no one knows the extent of it. Neither the seller or the buyer are going to bring attention to it. The enterprising criminal will use this fact to defraud the buyer. They pretend to have this data and sell the fake data. As it is an illegal act, the buyer has no desire to involve the police. This goes for all types of events where there is a database of attendees, such as exhibitions and conferences. A typical message from the event organisers is:

Please be aware of fake email and offers. These emails are sent by scammers impersonating the event. We do not sell exhibitor or attendee lists of any event that we run and any person claiming to offer our attendee lists is committing fraud.

As well as selling databases, the fraudsters offer to arrange personnel transport and equipment logistics and accommodation for the conference or exhibition.

> The vulnerable points for the events are the ticketing and any online registration, mobile apps and wifi networks.

The laws regarding data breaches vary around the world. Data breach notification laws require that entities, which have been subjected to a breach, must contact the individuals whose data was breached and other relevant parties and inform them about the incident. The laws vary according to the manner of notification and the time limit such as 72 hours. The laws for each country can be found on a specialist website Data Protection Laws of the World (https://www.dlapiperdataprotection.com/)

Data breaches can result from unexpected changes in the event planning. At one major music festival people bought tickets, arranged airfares and accommodation only to find that many of the performers they wanted to see had cancelled. These ticket holders then applied for a ticket refund that was available. Going online they were surprised to see a list of other ticket holder's names and contact details, complete with their bank details. This had to do with the online process of asking for a refund.

The U.S. Cybersecurity and Infrastructure Security Agency (CISA) with many other agencies has published a manual, *Mitigating Cyber Threats with Limited Resources: Guidance for Civil Society* describing how to reduce exposure to cybercrime.

These are applicable to event organisations. More detail is found on their website and manual. In outline the recommendations include:

- Keep software updated on user devices and IT infrastructure.
- Implement phishing-resistant multifactor authentication (MFA).
- Audit accounts and disable unused and unnecessary accounts.
- Disable user accounts and access to organizational resources for departing staff.
- Apply the *Principle of Least Privilege.*
- Exercise due diligence when selecting vendors, including cloud service providers (CSP) and
- managed service provider (MSPs).

- Review contractual relationships with all service providers, prioritizing providers of critical services first.
- Manage architecture risks by auditing and reviewing connections and using a dedicated VPN.
- Implement basic cybersecurity training.
- Develop and exercise incident response and recovery. (CISA, 2024)

The *Principle of Least Privilege,* according to the US National Institute of Standards and Technology is:

> *"The principle that a security architecture should be designed so that each entity is granted the minimum system resources and authorizations that the entity needs to perform its function."* (NIST, 2017, p. 81)

Story 23: Cyber pandemonium

1. The Pandemonium Rocks, a music festival, in 2024 had to reduce their event to one stage as a number of the headline acts cancelled. They offered a refund and the ticket holders had to go online to claim the refund. The glitch in the software enabled the names, bank details, email addresses, and phone numbers of 400 ticket-holders to be revealed.

2. Live Nation Entertainment informed the United States Securities and Exchange Commission that there was "unauthorized activity within a third-party cloud database environment.... On May 27, 2024, a criminal threat actor offered what it alleged to be Company user data for sale via the dark web". According to the press reports the hackers asked for $500,000 for the stolen information from customers. They claimed they had information from 560 million Ticketmaster customers, including credit card numbers and ticket sales. (SEC, 2024)

The cyber crimes illustrate an aspect of the risk of centralised systems. Petty corruption such as cash kickbacks and facilitation payments are often small and localised. Using an IT system for the management of events, such as the ticketing and credit cards, is efficient, however the risk can go from small and distributed to centralised and catastrophic.

The use of fake QR codes is so common it has its own name: "quishing". Fake QR codes in the event sector are used to gather data, obtain payments or other illegal purposes. One festival reported that their on-site signage, at the event, had been altered. There was a stick-on addition of a QR code and a request to donate. This went to a fake charity website. Another had their event website replicated with a request for the patrons to pay a registration fee to attend the event.

The centralisation solution to a distributed yet individually small risk, such as photocopying a ticket, may introduce a centralised disastrous risk. If the reader or student is interested in this aspect of risk management, Nasim Taleb's book *Antifragile* (Taleb, 2012) discusses the theory and practice.

Malice, stupidity, fraud or mistakes

To finish this section on the types of corruption found in the events sector, it is important not to hide behind more regulation. The simplistic solution to all problems is to suggest more plans and more requirements. However, I hope this book demonstrates that the future is about risk, uncertainty, innovation, opportunity and probability. Not simply about rigid compliance. Corruption is forever resourceful and every rigid plan can be gamed. Planning and compliance assumes we can predict the future exactly. The official response to every act of corruption has been 'more planning'.

It is interesting that the major change to the various international standards in the last few years is to rewrite the standards from the perspective of the management of the risks as a system. A system responds to changes rather than simply controlling them by developing plans. It is dynamic. As pointed out by Adam Simms (2021) when examining the 2021 update of the AS8001: Fraud and Corruption Control standard:

> *The idea of a system, as opposed to a plan, is that it brings together the strategies adopted by the organisation to combat fraud and corruption as required, as opposed to a plan that may end up as another governance document gathering dust. This is because historically, we have seen that organisations develop a plan and then 'shelve' it—not implementing it well, or indeed at all.*

The Maturity Model of the evolution of the events sector warns of the reign of the mega events. The laws, rules and regulations are made in response to the mega events. These now control the development of new innovative events. The result of this is to smother new events and ideas in rules and regulation meant for mega events. If you are in the event sector, it is important to realise most events started small, even the Olympics and the International football matches. Also the festivals, concert artists, concerts and conferences. They often start as an idea and get tested. The mistakes they make on the way, as they develop, are the way they learn. Were those three events described in Story 4: *Inexperience an excuse?* (p. 38) due to malice, inexperience or stupidity? We don't know, but we need a way for people to understand event management is a high risk profession, not something you do after attending a rabbit pet festival and assume it is easy.

Due to the size of the mega events, their publicity, repetition and centralisation, they are easy to study, so they get the focus of event courses. It is the same with governments. The laws are made for the mega events. This was obvious during the COVID years and the terrorism threat. The mega events will eventually fold and need to be replaced. But unless we have the smaller events being tested and trying to attract audiences we will be left with a social and cultural hole, a barren landscape.

This book is to ensure these events don't disappear due to the mega events. The next requirement without a doubt will be *"what is your anti-corruption policy" "can you give us an anti-corruption guarantee"*. With the new standards and their uptake around the world this is inevitable. Reading and using this book will get you there. It is easy. Most of it is common sense, events people know most of it and more than likely have experienced some of these types of corruption. But it is part of the dark side of events and too often no one wants to talk about it. *"Ignore it and it will go away"*. Not any more, the light has been turned on.

Summary

- ☐ Conflict of interest definition and examples
- ☐ Avoidance, disclosure, stepping back and refusal
- ☐ Extortion definition
- ☐ Consequence of other corruption - Story: Demanding money
- ☐ Reducing likelihood and consequence of extortion
- ☐ Favouritism, nepotism, cronyism definition
- ☐ Merit based recruitment and advantages of groups of friends
- ☐ Patronage
- ☐ Money laundering definition; placement, layering and integration
- ☐ Structuring /smurfing - Story: Mules
- ☐ Privacy/data breaches
- ☐ Ticketing
- ☐ Mitigating threats – Story: Music Festival, Live Nation

References

DOJ. (2024). *Fake concert promoter and former rapper plead guilty to $1.35 million fraud scheme.* www.justice.gov/usao-sdfl/pr/fake-concert-promoter-and-former-rapper-plead-guilty-135-million-fraud-scheme

European Commission. (2023). *Handbook of good practices in the fight against corruption.* https://op.europa.eu/s/xMzv

Financial Action Task Force (FATF). (2023). *Money Laundering and Terrorist Financing in the Art and Antiquities.* https://www.fatf-gafi.org/content/dam/fatf-gafi/reports/Money-Laundering-Terrorist-Financing-Art-Antiquities-Market.pdf.coredownload.pdf

Fox, T. (2011). *RESIST Resisting Extortion and Solicitation in International Transactions.* Paris: International Chamber of Commerce. https://iccwbo.org/news-publications/policies-reports/resisting-extortion-and-solicitation-in-international-transactions-resist

FraudSmart.(2024). *FraudSMART money mules warning.* https://bpfi.ie/fraudsmart-money-muling-warning.

Graycar, A. and Prenzler, T. (2013). *Understanding and Preventing Corruption.* Palgrave Macmillan.

International Chamber of Commerce (ICC). (2018). *ICC Guidelines on Conflicts of Interest in Enterprises.* ICC Policy and Business Practices, https://iccwbo.org/news-publications/policies-reports/icc-guidelines-conflicts-interest-enterprises/

Ivanov, E. (2022). *Overview of Anti- Corruption Compliance Standards and Guidelines.* 2ed. International Anti-Corruption Academy. Austria. www.iaca.int

Masters, A. (2015). Corruption in sport: From the playing field to the field of policy, *Policy and Society,* 34(2), 111-123.

U.S. Cybersecurity and Infrastructure Security Agency (CISA) (2024), Mitigating Cyber Threats with Limited Resources: Guidance for Civil Society https://www.cisa.gov/sites/default/files/2024-05/joint-guide-mitigating-cyber-threats-with-limited-resources-guidance-for-civil-society-508c_3.pdf Mitigating-cyber-threats 2024.pdf

US National Institute of Standards and Technology (NIST). (2017). *An Introduction to Information Security*. NIST Special Publication 800-12

Organisation for Economic Co-operation and Development (OECD). (2020). *OECD Public Integrity Handbook.* Paris: OECD Publishing. https://doi.org/10.1787/ac8ed8e8-en.

Sauve B. , Woodley J., Jones N., & Akhtari S. (2023). *Public Safety Canada: Methods of Preventing Corruption: A Review and Analysis of Select Approaches*, Report number: 2023-R010 https://www.publicsafety.gc.ca/cnt/rsrcs/pblctns/2023-r010/index-en.aspx

SEC. (2024). *Live Nation Entertainment, Inc.* www.sec.gov/Archives/edgar/data/1335258/000133525824000081/lyv-20240520.htm

Silverstone, H., Sheetz, M., Pedneault, S. and Rudewicz, F. (2012). *Forensic Accounting and Fraud Investigation for Non-Experts 3rd Ed.*, NY: John Wiley & Sons.

Simms, A. (2021). AS 8001: Fraud and Corruption. *The Journal of Family Office Investment*. 10(3). www.fsprivatewealth.com.au

Taleb, N. (2012). *Antifragile: Things That Gain From Disorder*. Random House

The Whitehouse. (2021). *United States Strategy on Countering Corruption.* The Whitehouse, Washington. https://www.whitehouse.gov/wp-content/uploads/2021/12/United-States-Strategy-on-Countering-Corruption.pdf

Section 3

Risk and Corruption

Let us turn on the lights as, in the dark, the cockroaches scurry around.

Zulu saying

阳光工程 *(Yángguāng Gōngchéng)*

"Sunshine Projects" used to describe various initiatives aimed at promoting transparency and combating corruption in China.

Sunlight is said to be the best of disinfectants; electric light the most efficient policeman.

Justice Louise Brandeis USA Supreme Court Judge, 1914

Just as it is impossible not to taste the honey or the poison that finds itself at the tip of the tongue, so it is impossible for a government servant not to eat up, at least, a bit of the king's revenue.

Arthashastra, Kautilya, 4th Century BC, Indian treatise on governance.

7 Risk management process

Introduction

This chapter is a review of the standard risk management process used in events around the world. In the experience of the author, it is also used in all other industries and therefore will be familiar to the event stakeholders, such as the government, agencies, sponsors and subcontractors. It provides a common communication framework for identifying possible problems across all fields. It is the proof of competent event management that is necessary for permissions, investment, bidding and funding.

If you are already using the process you can check it to ensure it agrees with the processes your events use. Corruption is a risk and the way to ensure it is dealt with is to have it as part of the overall risk management. It flows into different areas of event management and amplifies other risks. The risk management process must be known by all members of the team. Corruption prevention training (see Chapter 8) is part of the overall risk management workshops and training. As indicated by the quotes below, this is recognised by governments and anti-corruption bodies around the world.

According to the powerful 2010 Bribery Act in the UK :

> *" As the principles make clear, commercial organisations should adopt a risk-based approach to managing bribery risks. Procedures should be proportionate to the risks faced by an organisation. No policies or procedures are capable of detecting and preventing all bribery.*
>
> *A risk-based approach will, however, serve to focus the effort where it is needed and will have most impact. A risk-based approach*

recognises that the bribery threat to organisations varies across jurisdictions, business sectors, business partners and transactions."

(Ministry of Justice, 2011, p. 7)

The international anti-corruption training group, IACE, based in Austria, agrees and explains the role of the risk process:

"The aims of the risk assessment are to identify and assess the risks of corruption, to identify persons and/or structural subdivisions facing these risks, and to define and implement in an anti-corruption compliance programme appropriate mitigation measures."

(Ivanov, 2022 .p.19)

Finally, the United Nations emphasises the point:

"No risk management plan is ever adequate if it does not specifically include effective measures for mitigating the risk of corruption in its various manifestations."

(UN, 2013, p. 15)

The above quotes show the realistic way to identify and assess all types of corruption. With an event it is even more applicable because of the deadline.

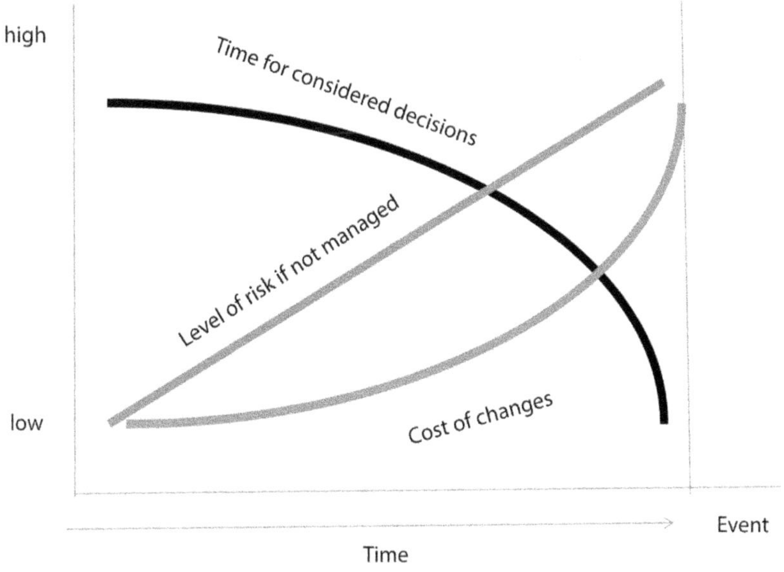

Figure 7.1: Decision /cost leading up to the event

As illustrated by the Figure 7.1: *Decision /cost leading up to the event*, as the date of the event approaches, the more costly are any changes. A risk that is small and manageable many months out from the event can easily become a disaster near to the event date. The lack of time to assess and consider issues can lead to the event management ignoring them.

The risk of corruption is an input into the risk management culture and plans of the event team. Almost all events around the world require risk management planning and the standard is the ISO 31000. The earlier version of the standard described a very usable method and easily understood table. This is now called 'risk mapping'. Needless to say, a complicated and technical risk management process is a risk in itself as the volunteers and new staff may simply ignore it. Hence the event must have risk and opportunity thinking embedded in all decisions. It must be part of the staff training and form the background to all decisions. As an aside, this is not a doom and gloom approach to management of an event. Risk is also opportunity. It introduces the concept of likelihood to decisions and stops the 'sky is falling' type of panic. It enables clarity and responsibility.

Risk management processes are fundamental to event management. The Event Management Body of Knowledge (EMBOK) has Risk as one of the five domains. The others are: Design, Administration, Operations and Marketing. (Silvers & O'Toole, 2021). The risk process, as described below, is used in all the domains. This is the common question known to all event professionals: "What can go wrong?" The overall process is illustrated by Figure 7.2. It can be summed up by the term reducing possible problems. At the same time it can also be exploiting opportunities. For example, enacting an anti-corruption policy for an event makes it more attractive to sponsors. As explained in Chapter 10, the companies that sponsor events are subject to laws and standards relating to anti-corruption. A company with outlets or branches in the USA or UK are subject to their laws, such as Foreign Bribery when it comes to corruption. Story 17: Predatory Conference (p 73) and Story 8: BHP Olympic payment (p 51) illustrate the extent of the liability. Also the sponsors are particularly sensitive to any negative publicity.

Risk analysis

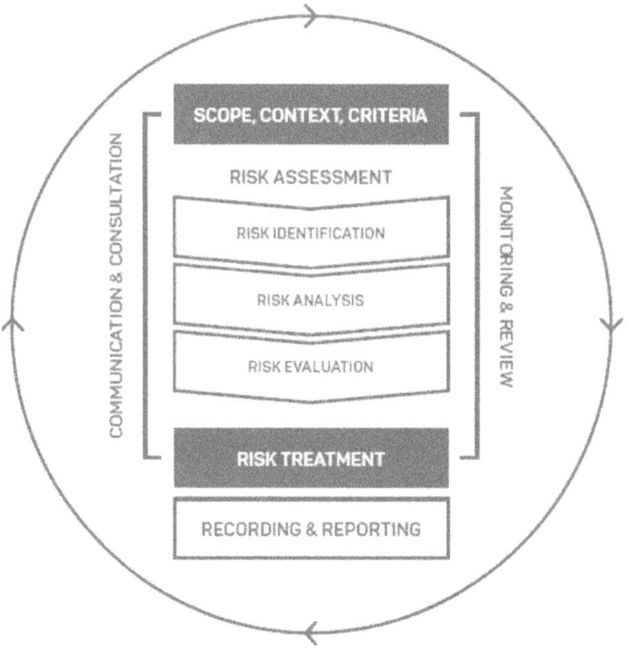

Figure 7.2: ISO 31000 risk process (O'Toole, 2018)

The process illustrated in Figure 7.2 ISO 31000 risk process from the government manual *Safe and Healthy Crowded Places* (O'Toole, 2018), is fundamental to all events around the world. The manual is available free online and can explain it in detail.

The risk identification and analysis parts of the process use the two dimensions of risk: the likelihood that it will happen and the consequence if it does happen.

- The *likelihood* is the chance of an action or incident happening. It may also be called the *probability*. It is estimated from past experience, historical data and knowledge.
- The *consequence* is also called the *result* or *severity*. It is core to risk management.

There are so many things that can go wrong with an event, the event team must be able to recognise and deal with the worst as the top priority. It is important understand that it is not exact and can change dramatically as the event project moves along. It is here that the event team should look for exposure points to corruption. Tables 7.1 and 7.2 can be used to assist in distinguishing these two dimensions of risk.

Descriptor	Explanation
Almost certain	Incident or situation is expected to occur in most circumstances.
Likely	Incident or situation would probably occur in most circumstances.
Possible	Incident or situation should occur at some time.
Unlikely	Incident or situation could occur at some time.
Rare	Incident or situation may occur only in exceptional circumstances.

Table 7.1: Likelihood

Descriptor	Explanation
Insignificant	Consequences would be dealt with by routine operations.
Minor	Consequences would not threaten the efficiency or effectiveness of the event and would be dealt with internally e.g. small financial loss, first aid treatment.
Moderate	Consequences would not threaten the event but would mean that the event would be subject to manageable changes e.g. financial loss, medical treatment required.
Major	Consequences would threaten the continued effective functioning of the event organisation and therefore the event e.g. major financial loss, important external resources required.
Catastrophic	Consequences would threaten the event and the event organisation e.g. death, high financial loss, major reputation loss, criminal charges.

Table 7.2: Consequence

Consequence is what will happen if that incident or action occurs. The consequence can be immediate and direct, such as the loss of morale or trust in the team. Also, in the case of corruption, the result may be subtle, hidden and take time to affect the event and its people. As demonstrated by the many stories, the ultimate result can be huge fines, the end of the event company and criminal prosecution.

Combining these dimensions allows the event team to understand the importance of the risk. From that the team examines ways to minimise the possible problem. It is foolish to believe that a risk will simply disappear. But it must be moved into an area that the team can manage.

The risk of corruption and the way to reduce this it fits perfectly with the risk management model. It is the fundamental theme of this manual. By using the Vulnerability Assessment table in Chapter 11 the event team can begin to analyse the risk of corruption.

As illustrated in Figure 7.3: *Risk and anti-corruption processes over the phases of management*, the planning, such as the governance structure, is only part of the risk management. Decision, negotiations and other changes will occur up to and during the actual event. Hence the risk management is dynamic. Once again a key characteristic of event risk management is time, because of the immovable deadline. This is shown in the figure as the phases of event management as described in the Event Management Body of Knowledge.

The first active step is creating the risk register. Not only does this assist the team in discovering and thinking through the risk, it is proof of competency in management. The risk register is also examined after the event to extract the lessons learned. It is a valuable feedback resource that uses the event to improve the future management of events. At the same time, it will uncover opportunities. It is not a negative process. All the Stories in this book contain valuable lessons.

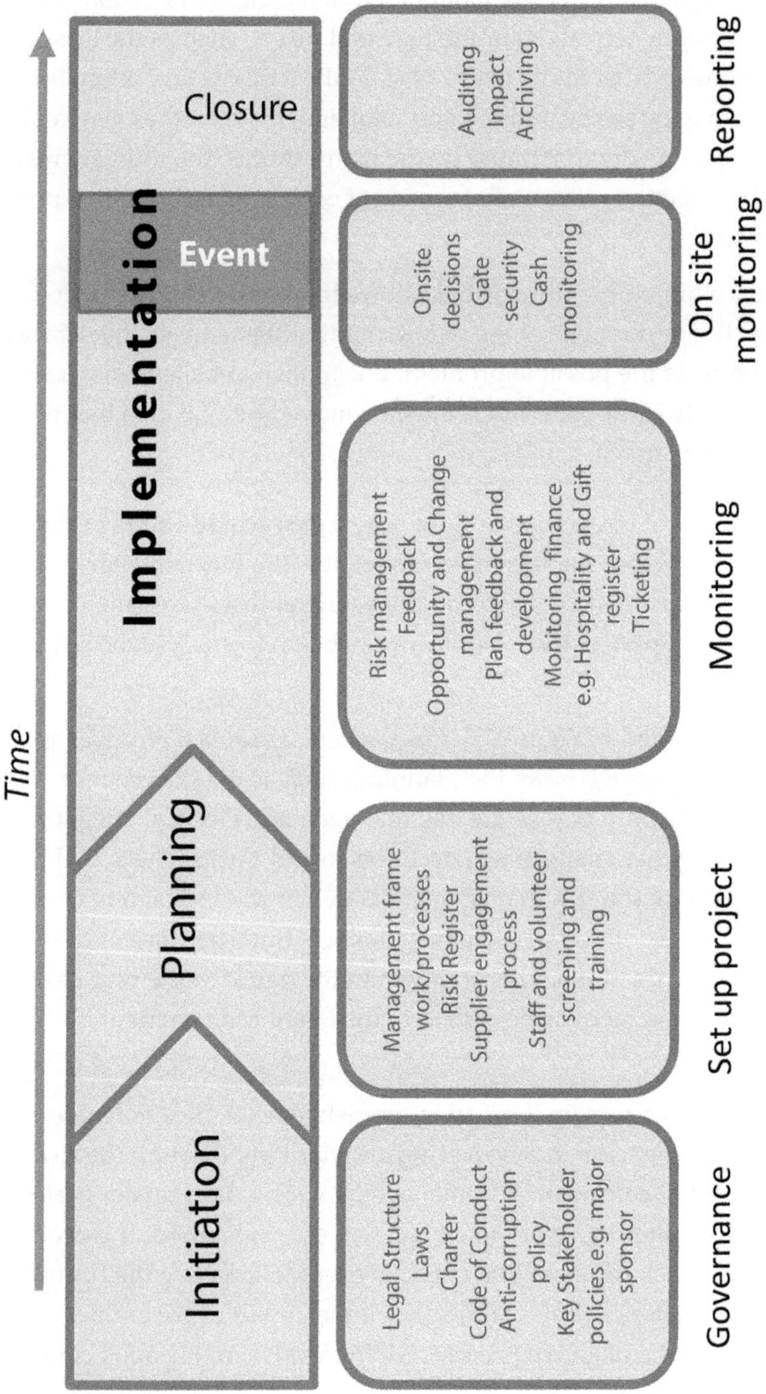

Figure 7.3: Risk and anti-corruption processes over the phases of management

Identifying risk, or finding the possible problems, is not straight forward. It must have an experienced hand involved as the complexity of events cannot be simply learned at school or from the web. To assist this there are professional tools described in the Chapter 9 on identification. These are real and serious tools used in risk management globally in all industry sectors and can be used by events of all sizes.

When a risk has been identified it is passed through the three tables. Not only is this analysis, it also clarifies the risk. For example a participant in the risk meeting may just suggest 'corruption' as a risk. Analysis digs much deeper. What type and when? The five dimensions can be used to clarify the description of the risk of corruption.

In the experience of the author these risk management meetings can easily go off on a tangent into imagined disasters. The three tables, combined with creating a risk register, ensure that the process works and people with knowledge and experience are involved. Likelihood is an educated estimate based on experience. In mathematics it is called Bayesian and a very well respected process of decision making. Basically it means 'you have to start somewhere or you start nowhere', then you refine the estimate. (Fenton & Neil, 2019). The process is:

1. Using the risk register: identify a risk,
2. estimate its likelihood,
3. discuss the consequences and rate it,
4. map it to the table and the diagram,
5. discuss and decide on the treatments options.

Risk register

The next step is refining the risk register. This is a table and is 'live', meaning that it is constantly updated as new risks are found and others are managed.

	Insignificant	Minor	Moderate	Major	Catastrophic
Certain	High	High	Extreme	Extreme	Extreme
Likely	Medium	High	High	Extreme	Extreme
Possible	Low	Medium	High	Extreme	Extreme
Unlikely	Low	Low	Medium	High	Extreme
Rare	Low	Low	Medium	High	High

Figure 7.4: Risk Matrix: note these ratings are approximate and can vary according to the industry sector.

This process can also be referred to as risk mapping. It is a visualisation tool and ensures the team and volunteers can understand the results and the process. Risk management must be inclusive. Even those with no experience in risk must be involved if they are a part of the event organisation. Depending on the size and type of event, this can involve the suppliers, sponsors and other stakeholders, such as government entities.

A version of a risk map is illustrated in Figure 7.5. The author has used this around the world to help identify risk and, as importantly, engage and include the event staff, government officials and volunteers in the management of risk. As it is easy to fill in and change, it reflects the ever fluid event management. In particular the sudden increase and decrease in volunteers, staff and contractors. The aim is to move the risk as far as possible to the bottom left corner.

The next step is the Table 7.3 *Priority and Actions* to sort out the priority of the risk. This must be done very carefully as a very small change in an event and the lead up to the event can easily take a risk from Low to Extreme. This table is to assist the analysis and prioritisation and it not a substitute for dynamic management and on-ground experience. ALARP is explained in Chapter 9.

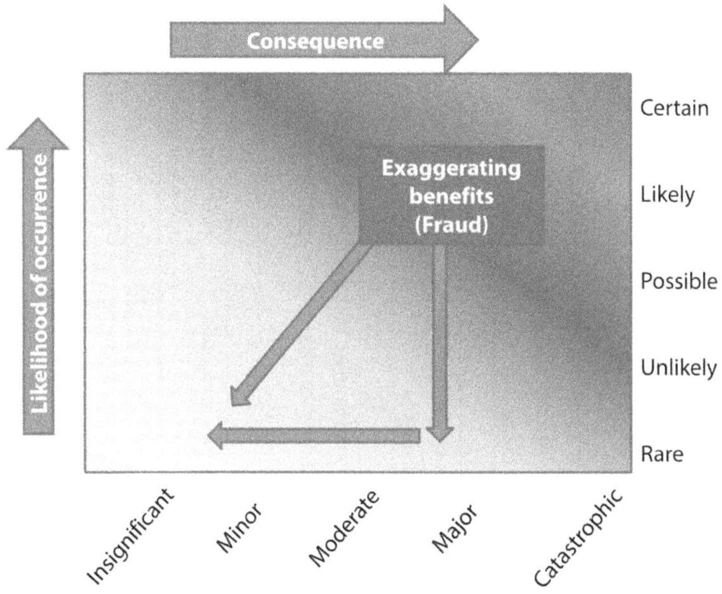

Figure 7.5: Risk map

	Extreme – This level of risk is not acceptable. Immediate and urgent action is required to lower the level of risk, such as not performing the activities/tasks that give rise to the risk. Any risk rated at this level must be brought to the attention of the CEO immediately
	High – Action should be taken to bring the risk as low as reasonably possible (ALARP)
	Medium – The event team will generally tolerate these risks but will expect a cost-benefit consideration of treatments in order to bring the risk ALARP
	Low – The risk should be kept under review. Otherwise, no further action is required

Table 7.3: Priority and Actions. Note: this is adapted from the ICAC (ICAC 2020) recommendations and should be reviewed for specific events.

To assist the user of this manual and students, Table 7.4, gives a sample of corruption risks. They are all real and have occurred. Many do not see the light of day as they are kept highly confidential by the people involved, to handle the possible reputation risk.

Initiation	Planning	Implementation	Events	Post event
1. Bribery				
Government permission facilitation payments.	Authority officials facilitation payments.	Kickbacks from suppliers.	On-site entrance. Access payments.	Overlook accounting discrepancies.
2. Collusion				
Event company colluding (fixing the bid) to ensure engagement.	Suppliers colluding to corrupt competitive bidding.	Suppliers only work with their recommended suppliers. Other suppliers don't reply.	Collusion to ensure best position on-site and squeeze out competition.	Doing a deal with the assessment company to hide risks.
3. Conflict of Interest				
Politician fast track funding for votes.	Event team members hiring their own company.	Contracting deals with friends.	Volunteers pushing their agenda on-site.	Positive impact assessment.
4. Extortion				
Secret payments for the right to hold the event.	Over paying to ensure collapse of event.	Demand last minute extra payments e.g. from performers.	Security demanding money or ejecting attendee. Border guards.	Politicians demanding a positive report.
5. Nepotism/ Favouritism				
Favouritism to event company by Government.	Hiring of staff planning involves favouritism.	Members of family get key jobs.	On-site jobs for friends.	Hiring friends to assess the event positively
6. Fraud				
Mispresenting the event.	Marketing exaggeration/ lying about benefits.	Ticketing, Chasing i.e. covering up lack of sales/funds.	Vendors under reporting sales.	Covering up an issues to gain more work.
7. Gifts				
Gifts to host to ensure engagement.	Gifts received for benefits.	Gifts to and from stakeholders, sponsors.	Festival as a cover for gifts to politicians.	Valuable souvenirs.

Table 7.4: Sample of corrupt practices in events

Risk Register										
RISK IDENTIFICATION			RISK ANALYSIS & EVALUATION				TREATMENT			
Risk ID #	Description of Risk	Impact/ results	Likelihood	Consequence	Risk Score	Treatment options	Preferred	Responsibility	Due Date	Notes
7	**Blagging**	Loss of revenue. Undesirable attendees. Later reputation issues.	Possible	Moderate	High	Inform entrance staff. Use "no bracelet no serve". Check all entrances including supply entrance. Cameras.	Inform entrance staff. Check all entrances.			Research other events
4.1	**Supplier collusion**	Increase cost of supplies. Quality issues.	Rare	Major	Moderate	Ensure proper competitive bids. Notice which suppliers are not involved.	Ensure proper competitive bids. Notice which suppliers are not involved.			

Table 7.5: Sample Risk Register. Note this is for training, the information and the headings would be far more detailed in practice

Table 7.5 shows the risk register. The risk register is used around the world in many industry sectors. The headings and the terminology may slightly vary. In essence the headings are:

- **Code** – this may relate to the management area.
- **Risk** – description of the possible problem.
- **Consequence/result**: a description of what will happen if it is not managed.
- **Likelihood rating**: from the table.
- **Consequence rating**: from the table.
- **Level of risk**: from the map.
- **Treatment options**: should be a list.
- **Preferred treatment**: from the options.
- **Person responsible**.
- **Timetable** for action.

The register headings can get quite complex. If so it may defeat the purpose of the register to identify, analyse and manage the risks. It is not an end in itself.

The most likely types of corruption ascertained from the Vulnerability Assessment table in Chapter 11 can be listed with the other risks and dealt with in a similar manner. The issue is of the scale of the consequence of the corruption as there are many 'secondary risks'. Knowledge about this is difficult to obtain as it is part of the hidden world. One reason for writing this textbook is to turn on this light.

Story 24: Short cut

There are many publications on sport and corruption. The competitiveness, the large amounts of money and the internet betting regimes mean that combating corruption is a constant battle. Lance Armstrong and the Tour De France is an example of how pervasive and hidden sport corruption can become. The lesson for events is that having any aspect of the event with the three characteristics: competition, large amounts of money and betting, is a red flag.

Marathons are a case in point. The rewards can vary, but winning catches the attention of the press and rewards can flow through other means. Here is a list from the press of corrupt practices:

- **Taking a short cut**: In Shenzhen China some of the marathon runners found an off road short cut through the bushes. Unfortunately for them it was seen by overhead cameras.
- **Luck**: In London one of the onlookers noticed the main runner had lost his identification number. He picked it up, finished first as he only ran the final 300 metres of the race and received the accolades and medal.
- **Slow down**: in the Beijing half marathon, the camera picked up that the leading runners were slowing down. This allowed one of the runners to finish ahead of the rest.
- **Face the justice**: the cheating is so widespread that facial recognition software is now used to ensure that the runners on the day are not a substitute for the entrant.

There are so many fraud issues with marathons that there is a special website discussing them:

https://www.marathoninvestigation.com/

Exercise

Examine a competition at any event.

- What are the opportunities for the type of fraud in the marathon stories?
- Put the risks in a risk register, analyse and discuss the treatment options.
- Is the treatment cost effective?
- Are there secondary risks or residual risk?

Summary

- ☐ Risk management is the process used tro identify and prevent corruption.
- ☐ The standard is the ISO31000.
- ☐ Risk has the two dimensions of likelihood and consequence.
- ☐ Mapping the risks gives each a priority.
- ☐ The output is the risk register.

References

Fenton, N. & Neil M. (2019). *Risk Assessment and Decision Analysis with Bayesian Networks*. 2nd Edition. Florida: CRC Press.

Ivanov, E. (2022). *Overview of Anti-Corruption Compliance Standards and Guidelines.* 2ed. International Anti-Corruption Academy. Austria. www.iaca.int

Ministry of Justice. (2011). *The Bribery Act 2010 Guidance.* UK: Ministry of Justice. www.justice.gov.uk/guidance/bribery.htm

O'Toole, W. J. (2018). *Safe and Healthy Crowded Places Handbook,* Australian Institute for Disaster Resilience (AIDR), www.aidr.org.au.

Silvers, J.R. & O'Toole W. J. (2021). *Risk Management for Events*. 2ed. Oxford:Routledge.

UN (2013). *The United Nations Convention against Corruption: A Strategy for Safeguarding against Corruption in Major Public Events*. Vienna: United Nations Office on Drugs and Crime.

8 Prevention

Introduction

The chapter focuses on the people of events. It starts by attempting to understand the corrupt person. Why do they do it? What opportunities are open to them and how do they excuse their conduct. Every day a person is presented with situations where they make a choice. Most people would not think twice about taking the right path, it is just routine. Are the corrupt forced into it? Perhaps it is at that decision choice that the risk of corruption can be minimized.

Next the standard prevention techniques are explored. Many of these are for ongoing administration and not for project based industries. However they can be adapted. They include:

- Staff rotation.
- Using scenarios.
- Event team, government officials and student teaching and training.

It concludes with a suggested agenda of a staff training workshop.

The prevention measures are the theme of the manual aspect of this textbook. They are found in Chapter 10 and include:

- Code of Conduct
- Event policy with clear reporting and disciplinary measures
- Culture of Integrity

The motivation of the corrupt

A model for preventing corruption behaviour looks at corruption from the point of view of the perpetrator. It is adaptation of the well-known 'Fraud Triangle' used in criminology and ethics to construct a more general corruption triangle. Part of the prevention of corruption is to look at the motivations and the opportunities. Note that ideology is included in the motivation. Some people will bribe, launder money, perpetrate fraud and extort others for what they regard as the 'greater good', stemming a future disaster or a religious belief. This is referred to as 'noble cause' corruption (Masters, 2015). The "everyone does it" excuse can be a result of perceived corruption in others or unresponsive management. It is then linked to ethical rationalisation that 'everyone is doing it' or 'it is the only way things can get done'. It demonstrates how corruption can spread very quickly.

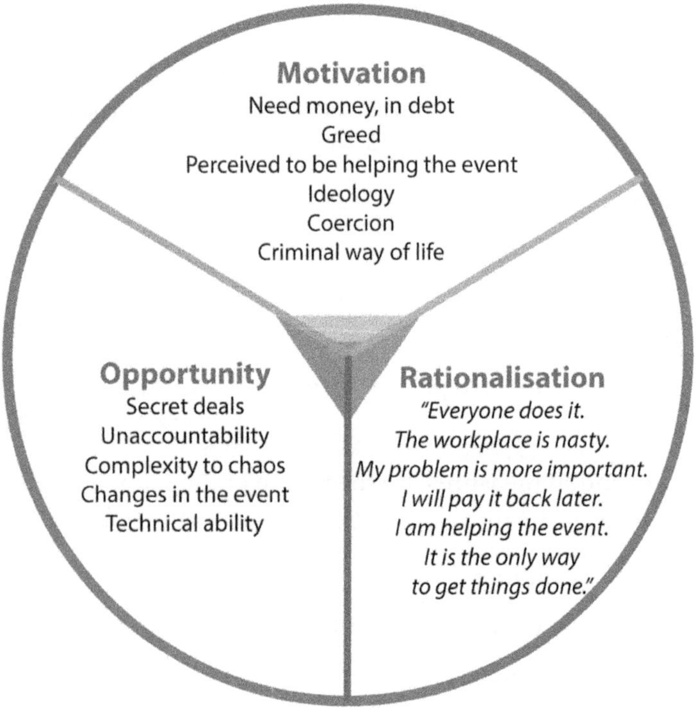

Figure 8.1: Corruption Triangle adapted from Cressey (1953)

The three key elements that often lead to corrupt behaviour in the events sector are:

- **Motivation:** This is what drives someone to consider corrupt actions. It could be financial pressures, greed, or even misguided attempts to help the event succeed. Sometimes, external pressures or a criminal mindset play a role. Coercion can include family or tribal pressure as well as extortion. There are cultural values and traditions that may motivate the person with absolutely no realisation that an act is corrupt. The person's ideology may regard corruption as justified for the greater good of humanity or a better future. It is well to remember that not everyone resorts to corrupt practices if they are in debt. Here we realise the importance of the culture of integrity and the morality of the team described in Chapter 3.
- **Opportunity**: This refers to the circumstances that make corruption possible. In planning and managing an event, factors like secret deals, lack of accountability, complex and chaotic environments, and technical capabilities can create opportunities for corrupt practices. This is related to the vulnerability assessment in Chapter 11.
- **Rationalization**: This is how people justify their actions to themselves. The quotes in this section show common excuses people use, such as 'everyone does it' or 'I'm just helping the event.'

Understanding these three factors is crucial because corruption typically occurs when all three elements are present. By recognizing these elements, event professionals can work to reduce corruption risks by addressing each area:

- Reducing motivations through fair compensation, team support, engendering trust and ethical work cultures.
- Limiting opportunities by identifying these points in the planning and implementing the recommendations found in this textbook.

- Challenging rationalizations through ethics training and clear moral leadership.

Corruption in events isn't just about money - it can involve favouritism, misuse of resources, or compromising the integrity of the event. As Brooks and others point out the triangle should be regarded as a useful checklist of factors rather than a science of prediction (Brooks et al., 2013).

Staff hiring and rotation

The event team can range from a few people hiring many subcontractors, to a full, yet temporary office of hundreds. Add to this the volunteers, community members and the personnel of the suppliers, such as first aid, security, sponsors, government operations people, sound and lights teams, police, cleaners and many more. On-site can include employees that are only there for the event itself. The recommendations found in some of the websites and books on anti-corruption are impracticable in a project setting with huge temporary on site workforce. For the core event team, the recommendations on hiring are to hire based on merit, fairness and attitude with clear criteria as to the position and responsibilities.

The 2020 OECD *Public Integrity Handbook,* describing the public or civil service, lists the advantage of merit based recruitment. Merit is a measure or assessment of skills, talent, competency, experience and knowledge. The advantages of merit as the measure are:

- It brings the best qualified – who may also be less tempted by corruption.
- It encourages transparency in decisions as these can be openly discussed and defended.
- It reduces the risk of secretly bought and sold positions and ghost positions (those that have no responsibilities but are a reward to friends and relatives).
- Meritocracies create an *esprit de corps* that rewards hard work and skills.

- It promotes a long term view of the job and skills with stability and possibility of advancement and moving to new events once the current event is finished.

(OECD, 2020)

When criteria other than merit are used, the person will always know there are people better at the job. This may mean they will be focussing on entrenching their position instead of doing their allotted work. This leaves them open to corrupt practices.

It is during the hiring and briefing of the temporary staff that conflicts of interest must be raised. This is dealt with in Chapter 6.

Selection methods that may include scenarios of corruption, such as accepting a bribe and the consequences. Role playing may be included. This may also test the applicant's integrity.

There are particular positions and situations that are vulnerable to corruption. For example, the entrance to the event site is an area of high risk for petty corruption. In investigations of the numerous terrorist attacks at events, such as the Bataclan attack in Paris and the bomb at the Ariande Grand concert in Manchester, there was a suggestion that doors were left open and suspicious attendees were ignored. Unfortunately this type of corruption can never be officially documented and, of course, can never be proved. (Manchester Arena Inquiry, 2023)

The other position vulnerable to corruption is the procurement personnel. Just as hiring must have clear criteria, the contracting of the goods and service for the event should have clear selection and award criteria. The nature of the event project is that last minute opportunities will be exploited and this is one of the glitches in the standard procurement process. For example, a few weeks before the event, a sponsor may decide to partner with the event. This brings in a new source of income as well as responsibilities to the sponsor. The extra income means the event can expand the program and attract more attendees. All of this implies an increase in the services and goods. At such times the integrity of the personnel is the most important factor. They must be aware of the implications of the quick fix on the event and the rest of the team. The risks are collusion, bribery, conflict of interest and favouritism. When working for or with the government, their procurement policies must be followed.

Depending on the type of event and the VIPs present, engaging a security company has its own issues. The secrecy needed for effective security is a hindrance to full transparency. But confidentiality is necessary for the company to function properly.

Although this may be unrealistic for smaller events, the United Nations Convention against Corruption in their publication *A Strategy for Safeguarding against Corruption in Major Public Events* recommends:

> *"It should also monitor significant contractors and suppliers, their performance and their financial situation and it should have a right of termination of contractual arrangements in the event that they are found to pay bribes, place themselves in a conflict of interest, or not comply with the terms of their contract. Contractors can be encouraged or required to do the same for their own supply chain."*

(UN, 2013, p. xvii)

Rotation of duties is used to avoid long term relationships and protracted incumbency as this is a source of bribes, extortion, conflict of interest, collusion and many more. The complexity of events and the trust needed for communication make this prevention method one that must be examined. Although the Canadian publication (Sauve et al., 2023) gives some of the empirical studies to support this as a method to reduce corruption, they do not concern the project nature of events and the need for personal trust. The event team should consider the vulnerable parts of the project and consider whether the benefit of staff changes outweighs the cost. It is well established in the security fields, such as prisons, to rotate the staff to ensure there are not long term personal relationships occurring. This also occurs at events with perimeter security.

Predictability is important to the perpetrator. Rotating staff introduces uncertainty. The other area stressed for the mega events is the procurement staff. Once again the personal knowledge, often necessary for hiring suppliers and dealing with the complexity in smaller events means they should consider the pros and cons of changing the procurement team. If the job is highly specialised the expertise and experience may be lost.

Another technique used to minimise risk of corruption is called the four eyes. It is based on the assumption that two people are less likely to engage in corruption than one. (Sauve et al., 2023). This method ensures that at least two individuals are involved in any sensitive or high-risk areas. It makes it difficult for any covert action by a single person and introduces unpredictability for corrupt acts. It is particularly useful at the event site. Cash handling and perimeter security are two examples.

Not all prevention techniques will work when the hidden basis of the event is illegality. The drug situation in the modern music concert and festivals is well known. This introduces a level of illegality that opens the door to other corruption. It is petty illegality in terms of individuals, but when added up it gives an overall permission for other corrupt acts. The physical sale of drugs can only work when security are looking the other way. If this occurs then it is no different to bribing security, theft of cash and many other illegal acts. It is fundamental to some of the events and hence there is little a 'code of conduct' or a policy will achieve.

One of the prevention methods is reporting. It is covered Chapter 4, but having a gift register set up can be a prevention technique. Table 8.1 shows an example of a simple gift register. It can be scaled to the type and size of event. Note that if the gifts are offered and refused , it should be noted as well. This may give people trying to bribe the staff or volunteers second thoughts.

GIFT REGISTER		NOTES
Date of exchange		
Name of giver		
Name of receiver		
Reason for gift		
Description of gift/hospitality		
Estimated value		
Reason for refusal		
<Name, date, position>	<signature>	

Table 8.1: Gift register

If this is a major issue at an event, it is wise to consult the more detailed analysis and guideline to this contentious issue in events in the manual *UN Global Compact Working Group: Fighting Corruption in Sport Sponsorship and Hospitality: A practical guide for companies* (UN, 2014). An example of the size of the negative consequences involved in gifts and hospitality is found in the Story 8: BHP Olympic payment (p. 56).

A note on red flags

A red flag indicates an issue. In anti-corruption theory, the red flag occurs when there is something out of the ordinary and indicates there may be corruption. In statistical language, it is an outlier. The problem in events is that the event itself is an outlier. It is out of the ordinary. That is the definition of an event. For sports event the surprise is in the field of play. The rest of the event: the seating, entrances, security, signage, food and drink is standardised. A person can go to a World Cup event in the UK, Argentina or Australia and expect the same. It is similar to conferences and exhibition. The conference and exhibition centres around the world are almost the same. The surprise part of it is on the stage, meeting people or a different exhibitor.

Other events, such as festival and special events strive to make the whole experience different, the food, the arrival, accommodation and even walking around the site. Hence many aspects of these events will be unique. A product launch that uses a swimming pool to launch an underwater phone is not an everyday occurrence. The dance of sails on a major city harbour of sailing boats choreographed to live music is unique. Hence many aspects of the event are going to be 'outliers'. Much of the anti-corruption prevention literature, such as Dominic Peltier-Rivest interesting summary of preventing corruption, focuses on the red flags. (Peltier-Rivest, 2018). This works when there is a continuous history of normalcy or a standardisation. Then, when money is missing or some of the suppliers never try for the job, there is abnormal situation and the outlier to indicate a red flag.

Story 25: Chaotic

1. At the 2021 Astroworld Music Festival in Houston, Texas, 10 people were killed and hundreds more injured when the crowd surged toward the stage during Travis Scott's set. The subsequent investigation described how many of the events in the region intentionally falsified applications or ignored the requirement of a permit. This was not the case for the Astroworld Festival, but the incident and investigation allowed the Sheriffs and County Judges to make this observation. (Texas Task Force on Concert Safety, 2022).

2. In August 2023 New York, the Twitch Streamer, Cenat, publicised a free giveaway event in Union Square. He was to giveaway free headphones, gaming chairs, video game consoles, PCs and keyboards. According to the police, he did not inform or obtain permission from the police or the city. The result was thousands of young people and a riot with 65 people arrested and damage to cars and the square. (Firstman, 2023)

That is not to dismiss the concept of a red flag, it merely takes it onto another level. The event project comprises standard practice and unique actions. Of course, it is not as simple as that, but the standard practice is certainly open to the red flag technique. The unique aspects need integrity as it involves independence and quick decisions. It is well to remember that mistakes are not corruption. The staff needs leeway.

A note on commercial in confidence (CiC) and non disclosure agreements (NDA)

One of the increasing barriers to preventing and uncovering corruption is the concept of 'commercial in confidence'. This is a catch all phrase that has been used to stop inquiries into the management of an event. It is often in the border or grey zone between protecting legitimate business interests and ensuring public accountability. Typically it is to protect information that, if disclosed, could harm a company's commercial interests. In the mix of private companies and government appointed event teams, it can easily be abused. The legitimate use is to protect competitive advantage and ensure the privacy of ongoing negotiations. However it can also be used to hide 'sweetheart' deals and make it legally arduous to find the truth. In the experience of the author, the CiC clauses are increasingly being used by government entities hosting events. The NDA may have a similar risk of allowing and hiding corruption by stopping any reporting or whistleblowing. There are laws that cover this, however in practice it can act to discourage reporting.

Story 26: Do the maths

The discrepancy between real and estimated crowd numbers was noted for many public events in Chicago. The event organisers must give an estimate of expected crowd size to obtain a permit from the city. The estimate is used to ascertain the number of police, security and ambulance reserved for the event. This is a cost to the event. The bigger the event, the more city resources are needed and therefore the higher the cost to the organisers.

"City law: the determination of the need for additional city police services shall be based on the expected pedestrian and vehicular traffic and congestion, considering the following factors: estimated attendance, density of area, size of area, number of street closures and affected intersections."

However, it was found that the estimate for one permit was widely different to the number that was used in its marketing and the actual number of attendees. The event company estimated 900 people for the permit and then advertised 30,000 to attract vendors. The number of people was around 5000. (Mercado et al, 2024)

Exercises: Stories 25 and 26

- ☐ Why didn't the event organisers obtain permits for assembly (i.e. events)? Is this fraud?
- ☐ Discuss the concept of compliance and its relation to corruption. Does it diminish or increase the risk? What factors would reduce the risk?

The Texas Task Force on Concert Safety make a number of recommendations on permits, such as a consistent permitting process across all the state of Texas and defining a show-stop authority.

- ☐ Does the bureaucratisation, such as more permits and more government stakeholder requirements of events, result in more petty corruption?
- ☐ Why did the event organisers underestimate the number of attendees for the city permits?
- ☐ What were the risks at the event as a result?
- ☐ What should the insurance company engaged by the event do in these situations?
- ☐ Was there a business opportunity in the situation in Chicago?

Anti-corruption training plan

There are a number of ways to ensure the staff are aware and able to deal with any instances of corruption in the event planning and at the event. The most effective is a short training session using the information in the book. The aims of the session are:

1. Definition of corruption and types.
2. Examples from the relevant type of events.
3. Why people act corruptly.
4. Understand the results of corruption including the loss of the good reputation for the event and the whole team – the long term risks.
5. Actions the staff and volunteers can take, such as discussing and reporting.
6. Typical scenarios for the type of event, emphasising changes leading up to the event.
7. Examine the planning and implementation timeline to discover vulnerabilities to corruption.

The training can be part of the general risk management training. One aspect to keep in mind is that seemingly simple fraud or bribery can easily lead to far more serious issues. Reputation loss, for example is a serious issue for a popular brand sponsor. These long term risks are too often forgotten in event risk management as it seems as though once the event is finished all the risks are gone. The risks, for the staff are not solely about the event, it can affect their long term employment prospects. The consequences of these risks must be well thought out and include the future for the core team, the event and the other staff.

Summary

- ☐ Fraud Triangle: Motivation, Opportunity, Rationalisation
- ☐ Staff hiring
- ☐ Merit
- ☐ Staff rotation versus loss of expertise
- ☐ Vulnerable positions
- ☐ Gift register as prevention
- ☐ Red flag/outliers and the limitations
- ☐ Training: using scenarios
- ☐ Stories: Texas, New York, Chicago

References

Brooks, G., Wash, D., Lewis, L. & Kim, H. (2013). *Preventing Corruption: Investigation, Enforcement and Governance.* Basingstoke: Palgrave Macmillan.

Cressey, D. R. (1953). *Other People's Money: A study of the social psychology of embezzlement*. Free Press.

Firstman, A.J. (2023) *Under the Influencer: Kai Cenat Charged for Inciting a Riot.* https://www.findlaw.com/legalblogs/legally-weird/under-the-influencer-kai-cenat-charged-for-inciting-a-riot/

Manchester Arena Inquiry. (2023). *Volume 3: Radicalisation and Preventability Report of the Public Inquiry into the Attack on Manchester Arena on 22nd May 2017*. UK: Crown. www.gov.uk/official-documents

Masters, A. (2015). Corruption in sport: From the playing field to the field of policy, *Policy and Society,* (34)2, 111-123.

Mercado, M., Ramos, E. & Victory, L. (2024). *City Street Festivals Are Underestimating Crowds By Tens of Thousands, Endangering Attendees.* (https://blockclubchicago.org/2024/08/12/city-street-festivals-are-underestimating-crowds-by-tens-of-thousands-endangering-attendees/)

Peltier-Rivest, D. (2018). A model for preventing corruption, *Journal of Financial Crime,* 25(2), 545-561. https://www.emerald.com/insight/content/doi/10.1108/JFC-11-2014-0048/full/html

Organisation for Economic Co-operation and Development (OECD). (2020). *OECD Public Integrity Handbook.* Paris: OECD Publishing. https://doi.org/10.1787/ac8ed8e8-en.

Sauve B. , Woodley J., Jones N., & Akhtari S. (2023). Public Safety Canada: Methods of Preventing Corruption: A Review and Analysis of Select Approaches, Report number: 2023-R010 https://www.publicsafety.gc.ca/cnt/rsrcs/pblctns/2023-r010/index-en.aspx

Texas Task Force on Concert Safety. (2022). *Report from the Texas Task Force on Concert Safety.* https://gov.texas.gov/uploads/files/press/2022_Report_Texas_Task_Force_on_Concert_Safety.pdf

UN (2013). *The United Nations Convention against Corruption: A Strategy for Safeguarding against Corruption in Major Public Events.* Vienna: United Nations Office on Drugs and Crime.

UN Global Compact Working Group. (2014). *Fighting Corruption in Sport Sponsorship and Hospitality: A practical guide for companies.* New York: United Nations. https://unglobalcompact.org/library/771

9 Tools of identification and analysis

Introduction

The Standard: ISO 31010 contains a list of advanced tools for identifying, analysing and managing risks. Most of these are applicable to the risk of corruption. Below is an explanation of how they can be used in this context. Although the terminology is technical, most event teams already use a version of all the tools listed. However they may be unfamiliar with the professional terminology. Using the ISO listing, the advanced tools are:

- B.1.2 Brainstorming
- B.2.5 Scenario analysis
- B.3.3 Ishikawa analysis (fishbone) method
- B.4.2 Bow tie analysis
- B.4.4 Layers of protection analysis (LOPA)
- B.5.2 Bayesian analysis
- B.8.2 As low as reasonably practicable (ALARP)
- B.9.2 Cost/benefit analysis (CBA

Brainstorming

Brainstorming means putting aside a time for a meeting during which the participants can discover what the risks could be for an event and places these risks into the minds of the staff and volunteers. The way to guide the meeting is to use the likelihood/ consequence table and the risk mapping technique explained in Chapter 7.

Convening a meeting of staff and volunteers and asking about what could go wrong is a key component of risk identification. It not only uncovers possible problem but it teaches the participants what risk is and how to analyse it. It is important that everyone has a say and the meeting is not dominated by one or two people.

In the author's experience, the meeting will focus on site safety risk. The reason is that these risks are often dramatic, catastrophic and can include the loss of life with many ongoing repercussions. It makes these a high priority. The emotional impact may take the focus of the meeting away from the cause of these risks. The meeting convenor should introduce other risks such as financial, sponsorship and corruption. These risks can lead to the on-site safety issues. They cannot all be dealt with at the one meeting. But looking behind the risks, such as a stage collapse, to what could cause it should raise the issue of dishonest conduct. These are termed 'upstream risks' . The next tool and technique listed in the ISO 31010 will assist in this process.

Causal analysis: Ishikawa (fishbone) method

Simply described, this is looking at a possible problem or incident and tracing it back to its causes and factors that exacerbate the likelihood that it will happen and the consequence if it did occur. The diagram resembles the bones of a fish and hence its name. By drawing the diagram through discussion at the meeting, the attendees can clearly identify causes and factors. A problem at risk meetings is that people will often go on a tangent topic that particularly interest them or where they have experience. The fishbone diagram helps to keep the meeting on track. It also ensures that the quietest people have their say.

It is recommended that 'corruption' be at least one of the bones of the fish. As mentioned many times, corruption is a topic people shy away from. It is hidden and needs to see the light of day. An example is in Figure 9.2. Added to the original figure is the issue of guarding the guards. But there are many types of corruption that would contribute to a drug death at an event. The illegal nature of drugs and drug use can, and you can be certain, that it does, introduce other types of illegal actions to an event. The sale of drugs introduces the need for some form of money laundering, for example.

Adapting the ISO 31010 description to events, the advantages of this method are:

- It provides a clear structure for brainstorming.
- It encourages participation by members of the meeting.
- The graphics are easy to interpret and enable analysis.
- This type of visual representation is common to many cultures and work methods and hence is inclusive of temporary staff.
- It can be used in many situations found in events and can include scenarios and "what ifs".
- It is neutral and does not diminish or judge the contribution of any attendee of the meeting.
- The analysis of positive and negative factors imparts this thinking to the attendees.
- It helps to identify contributory factors that may seem unimportant at the beginning of event planning but may well grow rapidly in effect with the slightest change.
- It is a deliverable of the meeting and contributes to the proof of active risk management by the event team.

One method of thinking through the issue is to use the process illustrated in Figure 9.1. The process is:

1. Issue is raised at meeting.
2. Risk is passed through the analysis and mapped.
3. Causes are listed. These are variable that will directly create the effect.
4. Amplifying factors: Identify factors that may increase the impact of the cause.

5 Confounding factors: Identify factors that may decrease the impact of the cause.

6 Effect: Refine the risk description and this may uncover further effects.

7 Sensitivity: Consider changing the strength of the factors and forecast the result on the effect.

Sensitivity analysis is one of the skills that comes with experience in events. Although it is a technical term from the engineering profession, an event professional will almost have a sixth sense about this. It illustrates the complexity of decisions in event management. If there are any changes the event professional must understand the significance of these changes to all areas of the event. Part of the reason for this book is to add to this sensitivity of the event professional by demonstrating the hidden, often long term, results of a seemingly small bit of corruption.

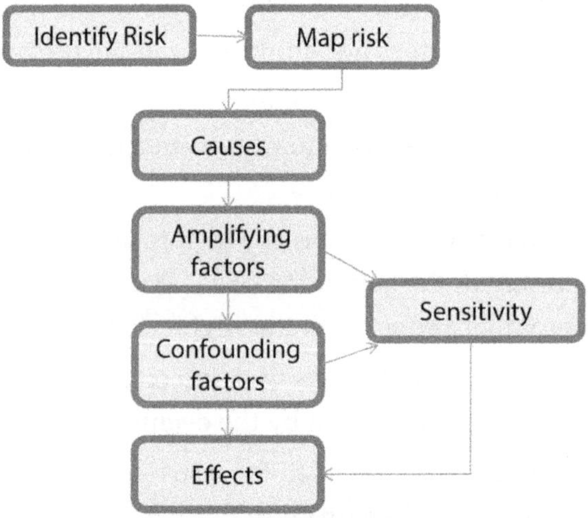

Figure 9.1: Process of creating a causal analysis diagram

The above can be used to create a causal diagram. Then:

8 Evidence/Supporting Data: ensure the diagram is supported by evidence.

9 Mitigation Strategies: Suggest potential strategies or actions to mitigate the causes or reduce the impact of amplifying factors.

10 Comments/Notes: Provide any additional observations or notes that might be relevant to the analysis.

11 Add to the risk register.

The limitation of this process approach is that the causes and contributing factors, particularly when people are involved, are often subtle, will interact with each other and may be covert. As well, there will be multiple changes leading up the event and these may affect the relative importance of each of the causes. Keep in mind that risk management is about managing the priority of the problem. A risk that is seemingly minor can quickly become a catastrophic risk.

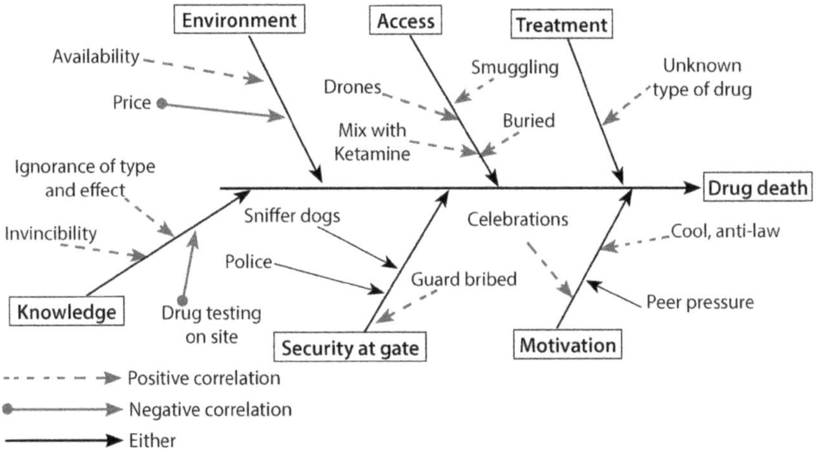

Figure 9.2: Causal diagram using correlation and origin for risk of drug death at an event adapted from O'Toole et al. (2020)

Scenarios

A scenario is an alternative view of a situation in the future. It is a hypothetical sequence or cluster of incidents and situations that could occur or may be missing. Scenario analysis refers to the discussion of a hypothetical future situation, attempting to discover the components, the effects or results, the causes and the contributing factors. At the meeting there should be an agenda that allows free ranging discussion and still keeps the meeting focussed on the future situation, the risks and the outcomes. It is an excellent teaching and training tool as the attendees will use their own experience to contribute to the discussion. For example when discussing an event, the students can use the events they have personally attended to add to the meeting.

A simpler form of scenario analysis is called 'what if?'. This can be used to introduce corruption prevention, by proposing, for example, *"what if there is bribery"*. However this question is far too vague. It is important that these "what ifs" are as specific as possible e.g.*"What if the guard at gate 5 is bribed before 10am to let in a group of five people?"* The specific question will allow the meeting to include their own experience. By focussing on a specific situation, the more general solution can be discussed. The more general the "what if", the more likely a person will say what they think they are expected to say. Any form of acting out the situation will help to loosen up the meeting and discuss the reality instead of the expected theory.

A meeting of event stakeholders, such as police, emergency services, public transport and the event team is common for the larger public events. These are called table top exercises. The technique often used is to propose a scenario, and to work through it asking each participant what are the risks and what are they going to do. It is very effective in assessing who is in charge if there are any issues, how the different agencies will react and any possible misunderstandings. Scenarios tend to describe a number of issues happening at once. For example; a child is lost, the guards at the gate have let in far too many people and there is a black out of electricity. 'What if' tend to take the issues one at a time such as *"what if there is a drug death at the event"*. Scenario analysis is used in a variety of industries to stimulate thinking about how to respond to various situations. Corruption, as it is hidden, can create the secondary risks found in scenario analysis.

The output of the scenario analysis meeting is entered into the risk register.

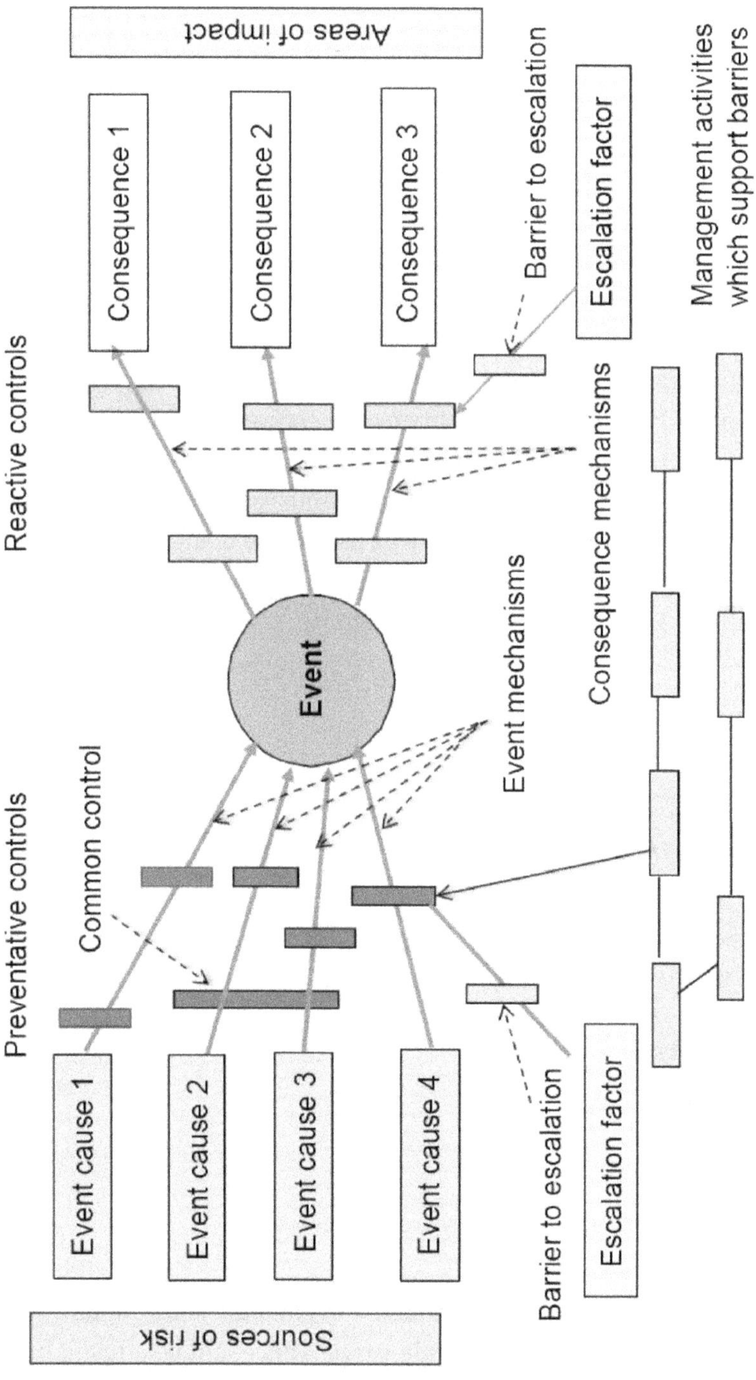

Figure 9.3: ISO 37010 Bowtie analysis

Bowtie analysis

The causal diagram looks for causes and factors, the Bowtie analysis furthers this by looking at the results. It identifies a possible incident or risk then diagrammatically lists the causes and factors, prior to the incident, lists aspects of the incident and to the right, lists the consequences. It is a structured approach to a major risk. It was developed in the engineering industries to identify and analyse safety risk, but can easily be adapted to the risk in events and more specifically the risk of corrupt practices. It can include the various control measures, and is a visual display that can be put up easily on everyone's screen or as a poster. Like the other tools of identification it is produced though team collaboration. The diagram can include the existing controls prior to the incident and the ones after the incident. This assists the team to monitor the controls throughout the event planning process. The ISO 31010 provides a good template for this exercise.

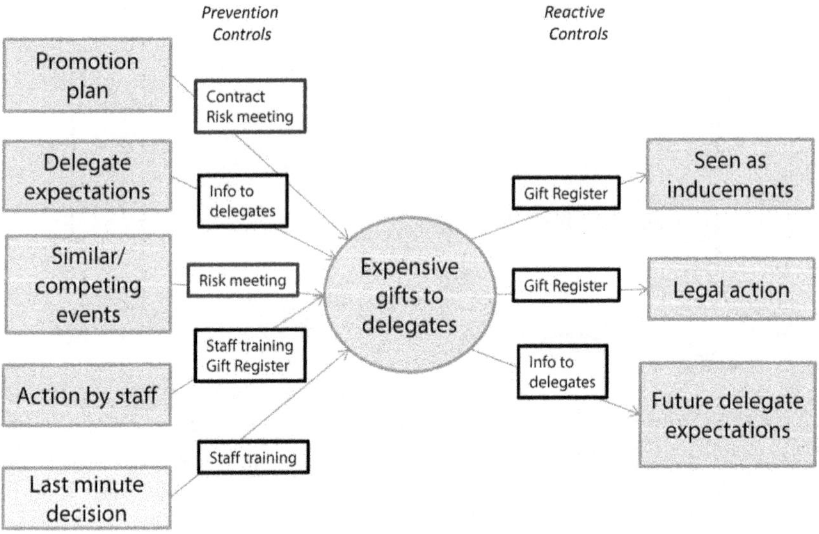

Figure 9.4: Simplified Bowtie analysis of gifts at events

Figure 9.4 shows a simple Bowtie analysis of the risk of giving expensive gifts. It is assumed that the event team is aware of this as a risk and has some controls in place. This could be a result of an over-enthusiastic marketing team without any knowledge of its legality or understanding of the negative affect on the event and event reputation. It could also come from the expectations of the event attendees. In some countries, largess is common and expected. Perhaps a member of the staff thought it was a good idea. The escalating factor is the both the complexity of pre-event decision and the time. Quick decisions often must be made and the consequence may not be thought out as the deadline approaches. A quick gift may solve other issues such as the need to attract extra VIPs or the attention of social media influencers to the event. This is a further reason to ensure the marketing company or at least the person in charge of marketing the event attends the event risk management meeting.

The reaction to giving gifts at the event may solve an immediate issue, such as number of attendees, only to move the problem to other areas such as legal. It may be seen as bribery. Also there may be reputation issues as it may devalue the ethical worth of the event, and trust issues as the staff will be more than aware that the gifts were not free but always entail a *quid pro quo*, i.e. a return of the favour. We can turn to the pharmaceutical industry and the medical conferences to illustrate how this risk diminishes the trust in medical advice and therefore compromises the credibility of the medical profession.

The Bowtie analysis is an excellent tool in teaching and training. To assist the analysis, a table can be constructed as per Table 9.1.

Description of risk	Likelihood level	Consequence level	Residual risks
Causes (list)	Current Preventative controls: … …		Improvements
Results (list)	Corrective controls: … …		Improvements
Notes:			

Table 9.1: Bowtie analysis prepartion table

Cost/Benefit Analysis (CBA)

The important tool listed in the Standard is B.9.2 Cost/benefit analysis (CBA) because it enables a clear way to view corrupt conduct. One has to think of the corrupt person, is the effort worth the reward? The event governance and day to day management must ensure that it is not worth the cost to the perpetrator. This can be linked to uncertainty – the greater the uncertainty of a reward to the corrupt, the greater the cost. Most corrupt conduct depends on predictability and certainty. The more uncertain the outcome, the higher the cost to be corrupt. One example we saw in staff rotation in Chapter 8. Ticket fraud piggybacks the genuine ticket sales. It relies on the expected predictability that a ticket will allow the person to enter the venue.

Once again, by using risk management thinking, the event team can find ways to reduce the likelihood of corrupt practices. This is not just financial reward, as the social rewards and ideological rewards may have to be taken into account. Bribing the security guards at an event, so as to undertake a terrorist attack is not a financial decision. In summary the prevention of corruption is about making the cost to the potential perpetrator greater than their reward. Ensuring that the staff can easily inform management on any irregularities, such as a whistleblower clause in the code of conduct, is one way to achieve this.

LOPA, Bayesian, ALARP

Related to the Bowtie analysis is the concept of layers of protection analysis (ISO 31010 B.4.4 Layers of protection analysis, LOPA). It may be called layers of prevention. This is shown as the controls in the Bowtie diagram. However there is rarely just a single control, particularly for the hidden risk of corrupt practice. Examining Figure 9.2, one can quickly realise that any one cause can have a number of controls. A single staff member making a last minute decision to give expensive gifts could be prevented by training, budget and fellow staff members.

The marketing company will have similar controls as well as what is written in their contract. In security and engineering this is also called the 'Swiss cheese model'. (O'Toole et al., 2020)

The other tools listed in the ISO 31010 that may be of help in the identification and analysis of the risk of corruption are B.5.2 Bayesian analysis, and B.8.2 ALARP.

Bayesian analysis uses probability. It begins with an estimate of, for example, *there will be nepotism*. It is given a probability such as 'rare'. This probability is updated as the event planning progresses when there are any changes or more information becomes available. For example, a successful concert decides to tour in other countries where nepotism decides who works for whom. The point here is that nothing is certain. Bayesian analysis, in its simplest form, reminds us that probability is an estimate based on our current knowledge and experience. It is never fixed (Fenton & Neil, 2019). Giving an estimate that an incident will happen is more realistic. Also the probability – or the more informal likelihood – as shown on the risk table 7.1 in Chapter 7, gives the relative importance of a risk. One must always keep in mind that corruption is within a maze of risks, all of which have to be managed. This aligns with the legal concept found in civil law: the 'balance of probabilities', discussed in Chapter 10.

Another term used in law is 'reasonable'. It leads to the next tool in the ISO 31010 list: ALARP (As Low As Reasonably Practicable). It recognises cost/time/quality decisions are made throughout the planning and the event. The reality is the corruption can only be minimised. The slogan 'zero corruption' may be a good marketing and motivation tool, but it is completely unrealistic. The slogan ' zero tolerance of corruption' is perhaps a better description. The acronym ALARP is used in Table 7.3 *Priority and Actions* in the ICAC guide to risk. According to the ISO 31010 'reasonably practicable' has been defined in legislation or in case law in some countries. It mostly concerns health and safety, however the concept can be used in the context of preventing corrupt practices. In summary it recognises that the risk is ongoing.

Pressure testing

Pressure testing is testing the internal controls that have been set up to prevent corruption. It is well known in the cyber world as the IT system is tested by attempting to hack it. The so called *white hat* attacks. Many of the recommendations for pressure testing are impractical when organising a single event. However, the large events and the event company or team may find this technique very helpful.

Pressure testing is a technique to find any weaknesses or gaps in the corruption prevention that can be exploited. It helps remove blind spots and challenge assumptions about how corruption is managed by the organization. As described by the quote from the Commonwealth Fraud Prevention Centre it requires thinking like a corrupt person.

> *"Pressure testers apply creative and critical thinking and look at processes and systems from the perspective of a fraudster. They do not assume countermeasures work effectively or trust that people will follow processes, rules and norms. Instead, pressure testers scrutinise processes and countermeasures by considering the common methods of fraudsters and applying an understanding of what motivates and enables individuals to commit fraud."*
>
> (Commonwealth Fraud Prevention Centre, 2020, p. 4).

The testing can be a combination of desktop research, meetings and observation. Analysis of information is the next level, such as examining the financial data. The final level is directly testing the counter measures. This is called *white box* testing – overtly going through the anti-corruption measure with the relevant staff or volunteers. *Black box* testing is covertly testing the measures. Here the staff are not told about the test, as the results could be contaminated. White hat hacking is an example of this.

Some of the vulnerabilities that may be found are:

- Staff not verifying information from suppliers.
- People allowed on-site without approval.

- Lack of reporting of minor corruption such as grease payments.
- Low or nonexistence of awareness of the effects of corruption on careers.
- Gifts being dismissed as 'how it is done here'.
- Private information on event attendees being loosely policed.
- Equipment arriving or leaving the site without inspection.

The recommended process of pressure testing is to follow these steps:

- Authorisation may be needed to start the process. This could include the event board and legal advice.
- Identify the person who will undertake the testing with the necessary skills. Creating and spotting fake invoicing for example will need accounting skills. Testing the back stage entrance security will need skills in standard security operations.
- Any covert testing may need special permission and legal advice. If there is a serious find the evidence may not be admissible in court.
- Develop measurable pressure tests with outcomes that can be reported without ambiguity in the findings.
- Ensuring there is recording and reporting of key actions, decisions and outcomes.
- Finally, ensuring there is a way to monitor the treatments.

(IPSFF, 2022), (CFPC, 2020)

If the event team needs to use the Black box method they must be careful to understand the legality of it. Deceiving people is not a good idea and has long term consequences. Testing an engineering system (which is where the concept came from) is not the same as testing people. It can also be seen as similar to attempted entrapment. Entrapment refers to a situation where a person in authority induces, persuades, or encourages individuals to commit a crime that they might not have otherwise committed.

Story 27: Gangsta Extortion

An investor company had placed a lot of money – over a million dollars – into a Gangsta Rap concert. The investor was smart enough to ensure the money from the ticket sales went to their company before it was handed over to the event company. Everything looked good as the tickets were selling well and there were offers to take the concert to other cities. The venue for the night had over 15,000 people. The performers arrived in limousines. One of the important performers took the investor aside and demanded a bag of illegal drugs before he and his act would go onstage. This is an example of extortion. Illegal in many ways and the performer knew exactly the right time to demand it.

Exercise

1 Use the five dimensions (p. 42) to describe the corruption.

2 Analyse this Story using the Bowtie analysis.

Describe the risk: the last minute demand for an illegal substance

- ☐ List the possible causes
- ☐ List the preventative controls?
- ☐ Could this be expected?
- ☐ What are the consequences?

Consequence

The consequences of corruption are found in Figure 2.1: *Simple Bowtie analysis of corruption and events* (p. 16) and in Chapters 2 and 3 on consequential ethics.

The first paragraph of the ISO 37001 Anti-bribery gives a good summary of the consequences of corruption:

> *"Bribery is a widespread phenomenon. It raises serious social, moral, economic and political concerns, undermines good governance, hinders development and distorts competition. It erodes*

justice, undermines human rights and is an obstacle to the relief of poverty. It also increases the cost of doing business, introduces uncertainties into commercial transactions, increases the cost of goods and services, diminishes the quality of products and services, which can lead to loss of life and property, destroys trust in institutions and interferes with the fair and efficient operation of markets."

(ISO 2016, p. VI)

Story 28: Sub-sub-contracting

In one of the countries where the author worked, it was almost standard practice to subcontract any work and pay kickbacks and bribes to the officials in charge. The sub-contracting can be repeated and the contractor would sub-contract the work again. It was not illegal and reached back into the history of the culture. The end supplier to the event is then the cheapest. Any local suppliers had to make cutbacks to ensure they made a profit. One result was dangerous events, as safety is too costly and is the first to be compromised. All of this combined to ensure the events sector was almost non-existent.

As the country developed their business sector, events such as exhibitions came in from other countries. The exhibitors demanded a level of quality they were used to around the world. To satisfy this, the organisers had to bring in foreign companies to supply the infrastructure and services, such as sound, lights and staging. This made the situation worse. The foreign companies did not train the locals as they would be their competitors in a lucrative market. The cost of hiring foreign companies was at least 40% more than the equivalent quality if it was locally sourced. The foreign companies charged a premium as they knew there was no local alternative and they needed to cover the uncertainty in doing business in this country. It wasn't long before the government understood the long term effects of collusion and kickbacks and created an events development strategy.

There is much more, such as exposing the event stakeholders and the event company staff and volunteers to criminal and civil legal action way into the future. It spreads rapidly and disadvantages the honest and ethical suppliers. The consequences of corruption are multiple, hidden and not obvious until well after the event, if at all. The primary result is the lack of trust. In asset management terms: it diminishes social capital. As it is secret, once it takes hold there is very little the event team can do to re-establish trust. If the event company uses bribes to 'facilitate' or is involved in kickbacks, they will be suspicious of all other transactions. It poisons the work and relationships.

Surveying all the documents in the references and relating this to the events sector, the list of the consequences include:

1. **Increase in cost of the event**. There will be an increase in cost if there is collusive bidding or quoting by the suppliers. At the same time there may be a decrease in the quality of the service or product. Even a small time bribe can increase the transaction cost across the whole event. Once anyone realises this is what happened they will have to be careful with any other transactions. Thereby increasing the cost of all transactions. On a large scale and adding up for many events, this is an increase of prices across society and is equivalent to inflation.
2. **Legal prosecution**. Money laundering and bribing a public official are obviously crimes in most countries. The other types of corruption may well be precursors to illegal acts. The legal action may take place well after the actual event. This was clearly illustrated by the BHP bribery case in the China Olympics. (Story 8: BHP Olympic payment, p.56). They were charged seven years after the act.
3. **Extortion**. A single bribe or a seemingly small fraud can be used as leverage by criminals to extort larger prizes. A person can never know whether a facilitation payment is a simple payment for service or it is part of a grooming plan.

Story 29: Exaggeration or lies

The consequence of a small exaggeration in the marketing can lead to disasters at an event. Store openings and special sales around the world have this problem. Often they are not organised by event professionals and hence the arrival of a large crowd will not be managed. There are many stories in the press about this such as the IKEA openings in Saudi Arabia and the UK. With social networking, the sudden arrival of a crowd should be expected at free events.

Opening a new store is an excellent opportunity to promote the store, the location and the products with an event. Often this includes giveaways and discounts. Everyone is welcome according to the promotion. But 'everyone is welcome' is a warning that the store needs some way of effectively restricting the number of people. Once again we enter the border zone of marketing. When does exaggeration become fraud? What is the intent? Is ignorance of the effect an excuse in law?

Exercise

Use Bowtie analysis to examine the promotion company or team members for 'exaggerating' the benefits of attending the event. We all know this happens and if there is a disaster, the company and the event will suffer the legal consequences. There are many examples of this found in a web search.

4 **Decrease in quality**. Bribes, facilitation payments, collusion and favouritism will ultimately reduce the quality of events and the force quality suppliers out of the market.

5 **Loss of integrity**. This is often presented as reputation loss. However it is far more. Morale is vital to many events. The training and attraction of events is the *esprit de corps*. Internal suspicion of team members is a disaster for communication and trust. Many events such as festivals, concerts, weddings, staff parties are a celebration and this must be felt by all the staff and volunteers. With a corrupt act the team is divided

between those who are in the know and may be complicit and the others. Words and actions suddenly take on two meanings and seem completely irrational to the people outside the select group. The corrupt person has not only introduced this virus to the team, it can taint every person in their future work as well as the future of the event company. Even if it is not exposed, there will always be the suspicion. In Australia it is called '*white-anting*' as the outside of the structure looks solid but the inside is rotten.

A well known example is the Fyre Festival. The saying "*it's too good to be true*" was very relevant to this event. It was mentioned online, describing the very cheap tickets for the Festival including accommodation, airfare and food. This indicates the possibility of fraud or the descent into fraud. When an event price is 'too good to be true', there may be secondary risks or unintended results or delayed effects. How would you know?

Summary

- ☐ The International standard on risk ISO 31010 gives a description of the tools and techniques that can be used to manage risk.
- ☐ The tools that are useful to prevent corruption include (but not limited to) :
  - ■ Brainstorming
  - ■ Scenario analysis
  - ■ Causal analysis (Ishikawa or fishbone) method
  - ■ Bow tie analysis
  - ■ Cost/benefit analysis (CBA)
  - ■ Layers of protection analysis (LOPA)
  - ■ Bayesian analysis
  - ■ As low as reasonably practicable (ALARP)
- ☐ Consequence summary
- ☐ Diminished Integrity, the long term effects
- ☐ Story: Sub-sub-contracting, Exaggeration

References

Commonwealth Fraud Prevention Centre (CFPC). (2020). *Commonwealth Pressure Testing Framework.* https://www.counterfraud.gov.au/

Fenton, N. & Neil M. (2019). *Risk Assessment and Decision Analysis with Bayesian Networks.* 2nd Edition. Florida: CRC Press.

International Public Sector Fraud Forum (IPSFF). (2022). *A Guide to Pressure Testing.* UK Cabinet Office. https://assets.publishing.service.gov.uk/media/636bd005e90e07618c412d31/Feb_2022_-_IPSFF_A_Guide_to_Pressure_Testing_-_final_Version.pdf

IS0. (2016). *Anti-bribery management systems — Requirements with guidance for use,* ISO 37001:2016. Switzerland: International Organization for Standardization

O'Toole, W. J., Tatrai, A., Luke, S., Brown,S. & Semmens, T. (2020). *Crowd Management: Risk, security and health.* Oxford UK:Goodfellow.

Section 4

Governance

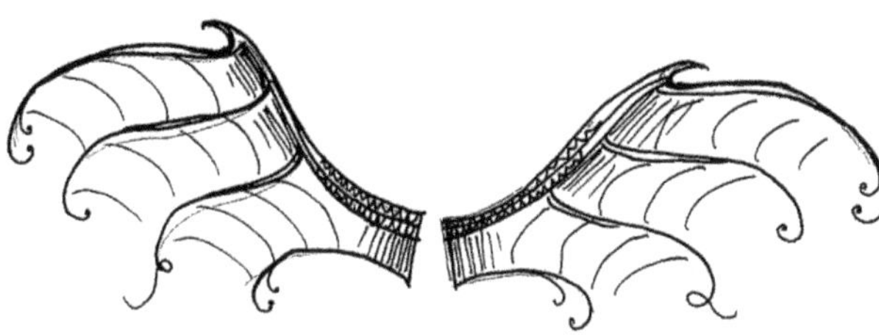

QUIS CUSTODIET IPSOS CUSTODES?

Who will guard the guards themselves? Who will watch the watchmen?

Decimus Junius Juvenalis 1st Century AD Rome

Those are my principles, and if you don't like them... well, I have others.

attributed to Groucho Marx 20th Century, Hollywood

But if they defrauded the Company to the Value of a Dollar, in Plate, Jewels, or Money, Marooning was their Punishment

II. Article of Governance of the pirate Captain Black Bart (Bartholomew Roberts), 18th Century

10 Governance

Introduction

Governance is the structure, processes, and policies that guide decision-making, management, and oversight of the event. It can be quite complex as an event is a project and the management must be dynamic, responding to risk, anticipating changes, looking for opportunities and keeping the work within the scope. Ideally it is set up prior to the planning of an event. However it must respond positively to the inevitable changes. The governance structure for events has two competing forces: stability and dynamism.

The governance structure may vary from private companies to government departments. It structure may involve:

- **Government managed**: Completely government managed event, such as a group within a department: In this case the anti-corruption policies of the public service will be enforced. In most countries these are clear and detailed.
- **Separate authority**: For major and mega event, such as World Expo, Commonwealth Games and Security Summits, a separate authority is set up and new laws passed to enable the event. Their policies and codes of conduct will follow the requirements of the country or city Government
- **Public private partnership**: in most countries these will come under the anti-corruption policies of the Government departments. Suppliers for an event are an example.
- **Privately managed event**: Many of the types of corruption will be illegal and others such as favouritism and gifts have to be careful as almost all private events have some form of

government relationship, such as using public land, government venues, legal non-profit structure, security, transport system. Any agreement or permission may have anti-corruption clauses. Also there are generally two parties to corruption and the other party may well come under the government policies. If the event is touring and crossing borders the company will come under international law with regard to corruption.

The governing body

The United Nations Convention against Corruption A Strategy for Safeguarding against Corruption in Major Public Events (UN, 2013) has excellent recommendations for the governing bodies of very large major events. This term is used to collate events such as the Summits, Olympics and the other mega sports events with key national government involvement. Although some of the recommendations can be adapted to other types of events such as festivals, conferences, exhibitions and the like, the scale of these events and the resources available make it impossible for an event outside that league to simply put in place their recommendations. For example developing and implementing a sophisticated accountability and tracking system or employing oversight, auditing and investigation agencies, is beyond the ability, time and resources of the average event. At the same time we should consider that these detailed and centralised systems do not always prevent large scale corruption. This was amply illustrated by the Rio Olympics. Despite all the corruption prevention measures there were arrests and corruption trials of the former president of the Rio 2016 Olympic and Paralympic Games Organising Committee, the mayor of Rio and the governor of Rio de Janeiro. Over 100 politicians were accused of bribery and other corrupt practices. It is said to include 16 kilos of gold bars hidden in a Swiss bank vault.

Regardless of the size of the event, the governing body is the entity with the responsibility and authority for the event management's activities, governance and policies. The management team of the event will report to the governing body. They can take the form of a board or a committee. However not all events have a board or committee, in which case the governing functions are part of the management responsibilities.

The leadership from the board and the team will set the tone for the event. Its aim is to foster a culture of integrity.

The recommendations, distilled from the various international documents, to prevent corruption through the governance structure include:

1. Ensure a culture of integrity.
2. Include anti-corruption as part of the event policy.
3. Establish a plainly worded code of conduct that can be understood by suppliers, new staff and volunteers.
4. Make certain the most likely types of corruption are understood by staff and volunteers.
5. Align the event governance with industry standards including risk standards and anti-corruption laws. These include transparent and accountable decision-making with clear criteria.
6. Ensure there is a person or group who take responsibility for the prevention of corruption and liaises with sponsors, partners, contractors and investors on these issues.

The major sponsors of an event will have a detailed anti-corruption policy. Part of that policy concerns the relationship with other entities such as suppliers, sub contractors and events. A risk for a sponsor is the event or partner is found guilty of corruption. The sponsor will expect the event to have governance that includes an anti-corruption policy.

The UN Global Compact Working Group Fighting Corruption in Sport Sponsorship and Hospitality has an interesting solution to this issue. This is to treat sponsorship as part of the supply chain. The processes used to attract, hire and contract suppliers, vendors and investors for an event can be transferred across to the management of sponsorship. The processes would include selection criteria, risk management, monitoring and due diligence, so that the sponsorship may be integrated within the system of purchasing. (UN, 2014)

Legal environment and the policy

This is not legal advice. For a start the laws, codes, standards, rules, regulations, local laws, statutes are vastly different around the world. And often different in and within states and cities and government local regions. To add to the confusion to the actual meaning of the words, there are the translations and the subtleties, yet significant, of cultural differences. Add to this that not all the forms of corruption listed in this book are illegal. They are morally wrong, but not illegal ,and every country may interpret that a slightly different way.

Given the above there is some excellent information about the regulations on various legal websites. How does this apply to the event team and the event? Due to the specific nature of these laws the event team will have to investigate it exactly. As to whether the laws are upheld or just for show, is an issue the event team will have to sort out. There is a subtlety here that is over-looked by many writings or websites, but is all too obvious to anyone planning an event. It comes to the fore when there seems a watertight system to prevent corruption, but the people involved simply ignore it.

It is well to remember that all the event stakeholders, such as the sponsors and any government agencies are well aware of the anti-corruption laws. An event team who is ignorant of this is not attractive to the stakeholders. The metaphor of corruption as a virus that can infect any one in contact is appropriate. No company or government department wants to introduce this virus via sponsoring or hosting an event.

	Example	Sample of laws, regulations, rules, codes
Interna-tional	United Nations	United Nations Convention against Corruption OECD Convention on Combating Bribery of Foreign Public Officials in International Business Transactions
Regional	European Union, Latin America	Inter-American Convention against Corruption
National	UK, China, India, France	Law of the People's Republic of China Against Unfair Competition, Criminal Law of the People's Republic of China, UK Bribery Act 2010, India The Prevention of Corruption Act 1988, French Criminal Code, Articles 433-1, 1 (active bribery)
State	Texas	Texas Penal Code - PENAL § 36.02. Bribery
Local area	Clarence Valley City Council	Fraud and Corruption Control Policy
Statutory bodies	University	NYU Anti-Bribery and Corruption Policy
Private companies	Red Bull Glencore	Red Bull Ring – Code of Conduct für Geschäftspartner Glencore Anti-Corruption & Bribery Policy 2022
Associa-tions	International Live Events Association(ILEA) New Zealand Events Association (NZEA)	ILEA Principles of Professional Conduct + Ethics NZEA Principles of Professional and Ethical Conduct

Table 10.1: Sample of the laws, code, rules and regulations about coruption

To give one example: Examining Table 10.1, one can quickly realise that a special event involving a government department in, for example, a university in Paris is subject to a cascading umbrella of laws and regulations ranging from the UN down through the OECD, the EU to France, the codes of the sponsors, the event association and the rules of the venue. All of these will have multiple clauses concerning anti-corruption.

No matter how small or large, no event is exempt. The purpose of this table is to demonstrate the laws and rules are multilevel and widespread. Navigating this for a touring event, for example would be almost impossible. Fortunately the United Nations documents on anti-corruption are the basis of most of these.

We begin the journey with the United Nations its *Convention against Corruption* and the signatory countries. Next the United Nations Office on Drugs and Crime, *the United Nations Convention against Corruption: A Strategy for Safeguarding against Corruption in Major Public Events,* the European Commission and the Organisation of Economic Cooperation and Development and the OECD *Convention on Combating Bribery of Foreign Public Officials in International Business Transactions.* From there we can go to some sample countries such as Australia, Kenya, Saudi Arabia and others. We'll end up with one of the best and well written descriptions of corruption and events: the *Audit Report 2010 Commonwealth Games in India of the Comptroller and Auditor General of India.*

The United Nations Convention against Corruption (UNCAC) is the primary international anti-corruption treaty. As of 2024, there are 189 parties to the Convention. Countries can become parties by signing and then ratifying the treaty, or through accession. Accession is a combination of signing and ratifying. Signatories endorse the Convention, while parties (those who have ratified or acceded) are legally bound by it. The UN does not impose direct penalties for non-compliance. However, parties are expected to implement the Convention's provisions, including criminalizing certain acts of corruption, which can lead to domestic prosecution.

The Convention applies to both public and private sectors globally, making it relevant to international and touring events. It covers prevention, criminalization, international cooperation, and asset recovery. Many countries have adapted their legal systems and government bodies to incorporate the Convention's principles and requirements.

The United Nations Convention against Corruption: A Strategy for Safeguarding against Corruption in Major Public Events is a highly recommended document for our purposes. It has been used extensively in this book. However it is for the mega events with years to plan and supported at the highest levels of politics with mega sponsorship and capital expenditure. The 'smaller' events the festivals, concerts, conferences and exhibitions are subjected to exactly the same anti-corruption laws and codes as high profile mega events. Unfortunately, as pointed out in the Maturity Model of events sector development (O'Toole, 2021), the mega events set the laws and standards. These same laws are not scaled down for the smaller events.

Accompanying the UN Convention Against Corruption is the Organisation for Economic Co-operation and Development (OECD) Convention on combatting bribery. It concerns international business and is legally binding to the signatories that comprise approximately 40 countries. Many of the trade agreements with groups of countries will have anti-corruption clauses. The aim is to level the playing field and ensure that competition is fair. The USA for example has the U.S. Foreign Corrupt Practices Act (FCPA). The United States-Mexico-Canada Agreement (USMCA) has a large section on bribery and requires all three counties to criminalise bribery. (USMCA, 2020)

As well as these regional and international conventions, there are international bodies, either government or private who produce guidelines and standards. These can also be used in a court of law to prove practicality and standards in the industry. In particular, the International Organization for Standardization (ISO) standards and publications of Transparency International.

From the international level we drill down to each country. There are many up to date publications on the laws of the countries concerning corruption. Most of the sites are aimed at businesses who want to work in the country concerned. Perhaps the most well known is the *UK Bribery Act 2010*. An important aspect of this act is that it is wide ranging and concerns any citizen of the UK taking part in bribery in any country, not just in the UK. Furthermore it covers any foreign company with operations in the UK.

Going back to Table 10.1, we can see we are only half way down the table. From country level there are state rules and in some countries, city and local authority codes, rules and regulations on corruption.

Story 29: Ambiguity

The director of a public event is responsible for organizing a large community festival. Various sponsors and supporters offer gifts, ostensibly to enhance the event. These gifts include:

- ☐ High-end electronic equipment (e.g., tablets, speakers)
- ☐ Luxury items (e.g., designer watches, jewellery)
- ☐ Gift cards to exclusive restaurants and stores
- ☐ VIP passes to other events and attractions

The director, instead of using these gifts for the event or as prizes for attendees, decides to keep some of them for personal use. They justify this by reasoning that the gifts were given to them as the event organizer, not specifically to the event itself.

Supposed charities and good causes can often disguise corruption. The event, in this case sold tickets to the audience for a good cause. There was no follow up as to where the funds went.

To conclude this brief legal overview, it's crucial to address a common misconception. Many people believe that evidence of corruption must be absolutely conclusive for a successful prosecution to begin. However, the inherently secretive nature of corruption needs a different approach. In some countries, the law recognizes that corruption operates in the shadows, making it difficult to gather solid proof. As a result, the legal system allows for some flexibility in the standard of evidence required. Investigators will rely on probability to build their cases, rather than always requiring direct, indisputable proof. Once assessing the probability, the case is passed to the prosecution. This approach balances the need to combat corruption with the practical difficulties of obtaining evidence in such covert activities. As the Independent Commission Against Corruption (ICAC) states:

> *"In determining whether a person has engaged in corrupt conduct, ICAC makes findings of fact based on the civil standard of proof (on the balance of probabilities) rather than the criminal standard of proof (beyond reasonable doubt)."* (Roth, 2013, p. 2)

Event policy

An anti-corruption policy's main purpose is to set the basic approach to controlling fraud and corruption, rather than specifying detailed controls and behavioural expectations.

The aim of the policy is to establish the basis for preventing corruption. It does not describe specific processes. It should set the tone and come from the leader of the event team. It should have a broad approach showing the ultimate results of corruption such as the loss of trust in the team members, the effect on sponsors and the loss of any good reputation that the team, the event and the company has built up conscientiously over the years. The major sponsors of an event will have their own policy and most likely this will require any event they sponsor to establish one. This is particularly true of international companies who are subject to the laws in the USA and UK because they have dealings with these countries. An example of this is Story 8: *BHP Olympic Payment* (p. 56). Having an anti-corruption policy makes the event far more attractive to sponsors.

The policy can include the commitment of the event team to prevent corruption and the people or the role of the person who will manage it. It may also include what standards or references are used to guide the overall process, such as the ISO 31000 Risk Management standard.

Policy template

There are many reasons for an event to have an anti-corruption policy. The first and foremost is that when the staff or volunteers are approached they can immediately refer to the policy of the event. This takes it out of the personal and places the request into the public sphere. This can help kill the virus before it starts. As emphasised in this book, seemingly small act of corruption can have wide and long term effects.

The policy emphasises to the team that there is such a thing as corruption and that events are a prime target. Many event personnel, particularly community volunteers, have no experience of this type of behaviour. They have joined the event for the thrill and camaraderie. They have never met the Geryon.

Using the template below it is straightforward for any event to adapt it to their circumstances. It is presented as headings to fill out. A policy, just like the risk register, should never be simply copied from other events. Despite the quick fix for a contract requirement viz "*the event company must have an anti-corruption policy*", this box ticking is dangerous as it helps to keep any corruption well hidden. It also demonstrates to staff that the 'quick fix' is a technique they can use and diminishes the ethical basis of good management. It is a facade of compliance that does not address actual corruption and makes it harder to detect the real thing.

The name of the document can include fraud and bribery. This will be dependent on the type of event and the jurisdiction. For example it would be wise for an event crossing many borders to have bribery in its title, such as *Anti-Bribery Policy.*

The headings of the Policy can be:

Definitions: Not all the staff understands the concept of corruption and listing the types of corruption will assist them. Event examples will help them to contextualise the list.

Relevant acts, rules and regulations: As this part can be quite complex, a summary of these with a link for more information.

Awareness and responsibility of all staff including volunteers: vigilance, raising concern.

This can be done during risk management meetings and if seen as likely the tools in Chapter 9: Tools of identification and analysis, can be employed. In particular, scenario development will help them work though a situation where they are asked or witness an instance.

Expectations of the staff, volunteers and subcontractors honesty, transparency.

This is an ethical statement for the event. At the same time this applies to the senior management. Leading by example is perhaps the most powerful tool in event management.

Dealing with subcontractors, gift giving, kickbacks and facilitation payments: This deals with the vulnerable areas of the event. Filling out Chapter 11: *Vulnerability Assessment* will help to find these. The petty corruption should be addressed as it may involve volunteers and on site staff including. "What to do if approached."

Identification and exposure of corruption – the process.

Outline of who will monitor this aspect of risk management. It will depend on the risk management assessment whether it is part of another responsibility such as the safety officer, a "compliance officer" or the risk person.

Consequence: This can cover: losing trust and integrity, extra costs and the possibility of extortion. Also reprimands, formal warnings, demotions, the termination of the contract of employment and it could lead to criminal charges in the future.

Figures 10.1 and 10.2 are samples of policies of an event association and a local authority.

According to the International Organization for Standardization, Anti-bribery management systems, the policy should be available as a document and communicated in the languages of the event stakeholders if the risk is above a low risk. (ISO, 2016)

Anti-bribery policy

Top management shall establish, maintain and review an anti-bribery policy that:

- ☐ prohibits bribery;
- ☐ requires compliance with anti-bribery laws that are applicable to the organization;
- ☐ is appropriate to the purpose of the organization;
- ☐ provides a framework for setting, reviewing and achieving anti-bribery objectives;
- ☐ includes a commitment to satisfy anti-bribery management system requirements;
- ☐ encourages raising concerns in good faith, or on the basis of a reasonable belief in confidence;
- ☐ without fear of reprisal;
- ☐ includes a commitment to continual improvement of the anti-bribery management system;
- ☐ explains the authority and independence of the anti-bribery compliance function;
- ☐ explains the consequences of not complying with the anti-bribery policy.

Figure 10.1: Example of an anti-bribery policy for sports organisations

The management team should:

- ☐ take a risk management approach to the prevention, detection, and investigation of fraudulent and corrupt conduct, in accordance with the effective fraud control system of the state government;
- ☐ reduce or remove the potential for fraudulent or corrupt conduct on the part of its employees, contractors, clients and suppliers;

- ☐ detect fraudulent or corrupt conduct through the systematic processes;
- ☐ investigate or otherwise formally enquire into all instances of suspected fraudulent or corrupt conduct exposed as a result of the detection processes, or as a result of receiving an allegation of fraudulent or corrupt activities;
- ☐ manage, discipline or facilitate the prosecution of those responsible for incidents of fraud and corruption as appropriate;
- ☐ ensure the continuing organisational integrity and transparency of its operations.

Figure 10.2: Example of a fraud and corruption control policy of a local authority or council

A culture of integrity

The leadership team must set the tone for the entire organization and foster a culture of integrity in which bribery and corruption are unacceptable.

The event team should be aware of the risk of corruption when entering into event partnership relationships. Most major sponsors will have anti-corruption policies. This is also an opportunity to fine tune the event team's codes, policy and monitoring methods with regards to anti-corruption.

The event team can also look for integrity guarantees. This is similar to the old guilds, whereby membership of the guild guaranteed a certain level of quality and service. The modern version of this is the association and endorsement by the professional association. The association has a code of conduct that should ensure the integrity of their members. However, this assumes that it is enforced with a penalty, such as expulsion.

As well as the membership of an association, other recommendations to predict the level of integrity in a subcontractor, staff or volunteer are:

- Background checks and checks with other people in the events sector.
- Their past work on events.
- What ifs and scenarios that include the 'soft skills' of teamwork, communication and reporting procedures.
- Testing the volunteer or staff in a role on a low vulnerable aspect of the event.
- Informal discussions in a relaxed atmosphere with the team and other volunteers.

A more reflexive way to do this is to ask the recruit how the integrity of a new volunteer or staff can be ascertained and how the current code of conduct for the event may be improved. This involves the recruit in the process of integrity and is difficult to scam.

Professor Adam Graycar, in his *Corruption: Classification and analysis* (2015, p.95), takes this further:

> *"The cultures of corruption can be addressed by focussing on major system wide pillars of integrity. The process and events that are corrupted can be addressed not only by focussing on integrity measures, but also by focussing on situational prevention measures."*

There is a simple cost-benefit judgement with regard to a culture of integrity. In the words of Professor Maesschalck when referring to the public sector:

> *"In sum, it is better to pay sufficient attention to integrity management in advance, than to be forced, after the fact, to spend much more to prosecute corruption and repair unjust decisions or to control the damage to the public sector's image. "*

(Maesschalck, 2008. p.16)

Story 30: Olympics

According to the UN document *"A Strategy for Safeguarding against Corruption in Major Public Events"*:

"In Brazil, the World Cup Management Committee, the CGCOPA, was established to provide a governance structure for the organization of the event. Twenty-five ministries and secretariats with ministerial status are part of the CGCOPA. The structure includes the World Cup Executive Board (GECOPA) responsible for coordinating and consolidating all activities, establishing goals, and monitoring the implementation of the Integrated Strategic Plan for the 2014 World Cup. For the 2016 Olympic Games in Rio, the Public Olympic Authority (APO) was created by the Brazilian Government. The APO coordinates the participation of the Federal Government, the State of Rio de Janeiro and the Municipality of Rio de Janeiro in the preparation and organization of the Games (with reference to undertakings made by each party to the International Olympic Committee and the International Paralympic Committee). The APO's bylaws establish the Authority's structure, its attributions and prerogatives, the operation and management of its related bodies, personnel arrangements and its budgetary and financial arrangements."

(UN, 2013, p. 11)

Exercise

- ☐ Research the 2016 Rio Olympics and the corruption that was uncovered. Their corruption prevention measures were based on the experience of Olympic committees around the world, combined with the other mega events and the knowledge and experience of the United Nations.
- ☐ What went wrong?
- ☐ Did the day to day petty corruption in Brazil create an environment whereby the mega corruption was normalised? If the day

to day laws on corruption are ignored, would the special laws and processes of the UN document quoted, to prevent corruption, be obeyed?

- ☐ To assist the process of discovery, causality and consequence, consider constructing a Bowtie Analysis diagram on each aspect of the corruption. Use this to find the commonalties and construct a general corruption causal diagram.

The Code of Conduct

According to the International Anti-Corruption Academy in their Overview of Anti-Corruption Compliance Standards and Guidelines:

> *"The Code of Conduct is a cornerstone for an effective anti-corruption compliance programme. The Code defines main ethical principles and corporate values, positions of shareholders"*

(Ivanov, 2022, p. 25)

The code of conduct is an approved set of guidelines for the members of the event team, volunteers and, possibly, attendees concerning their behaviour. It describes the standards that are expected. Ethical principles and professional standards are the core of the code. It therefore forms part of the prevention of corruption. An example would be conflict of interest. It may also include the process of dealing with misconduct and a discrete reporting process concerning corrupt practices.

The code of conduct is a form of self-regulation against the background of the laws. The code assists the event organisation comply with legal obligations. It assists the staff and volunteers in resisting attempts at extortion or solicitation of bribes.

The event team can create their own code of conduct or adapt a code of conduct from their major sponsor. If it is a government event, then it will probably already exist. It is wise to ensure it works for the type of event and size of the event. As people may come on board for the event days before it starts, the code must be applicable, useable, readable and understood. It should never be dismissed as yet another irrelevant requirement. Every effort should be made to make certain it is understood by all members of the team. It is important as it describes the integrity needed to combat corruption. As well it can be used as a defence by a staff member if they are approached with a bribe.

Many festivals and conferences have a code of conduct, particularly if they have volunteers. The volunteers can come to the event with a variety of experiences and perhaps subtle differences in ethical standards. This reflects the pulsating and temporary nature of the event workforce. It can quickly go from a few people to hundred over a period of a few weeks. They need a guide for their behaviour at the event. It can also cover the suppliers, vendors, staff and the attendees. It can have a positive tone, emphasising what should be done or a negative one, listing the inappropriate behaviours that will not be tolerated.

The themes include:

- Safety
- Attitude
- Respect
- Discipline
- Behaviour
- Communication
- Reporting breaches of the Code of Conduct
- Enforcement

Enforcement may include the levels that very in intensity from correction, warning, restricting to outright banning and legal charges.

Depending on the type of event, the types of corruption may be included in the code of conduct to help the staff and volunteers realise it is a risk. On site cash 'facilitation' payments is one example. The code must be relevant and understandable to the on-site temporary staff and volunteers who may have little time for training. A complex detailed document may look thorough but is unlikely to be read or acted upon by people who are only engaged for less than a week and unpaid.

The United Nations Convention against Corruption recommendation on governance of an event are:

- Accountable structure for the event team management of the event.
- Clear decision making processes.
- An external oversight body. *This can be adapted to events to have a member of the team responsible for emerging risks that include instances of corruption.*
- Policies that reflect the legal and best practices of the industry and region.

Similar to an event policy, the code of conduct could be supported by typical examples, scenarios and 'what ifs' of ethical situations and corruption.

These issues have been in the sports arena for many years and the events sector can learn from them. Even then the sports sector has not solved the problem of ignorance. As the United Nations point out in *Fighting Corruption in Sport Sponsorship and Hospitality*:

> *"The Sport Entity may also have a lack of awareness and knowledge concerning anti-corruption practices. Possible lack of awareness can add to the challenge that some Sport Entities do not subject themselves to general good governance procedures"*

(UN Global Compact Working Group, 2014, p. 12)

It is highly likely that the event stakeholders, such as government and sponsors, will have a code of conduct as well as a policy. Once again we return to the pervasiveness of the policy and code of conduct over the last years. There is no doubt that the various standards and codes recommend that the companies and department only work with companies, such as the event organisation, that have a similar arrangement to combat corruption. Regardless of its effectiveness, it is becoming a requirement. The appendix contains a template and some ideas that can help the event organisation develop their own code of conduct.

Reporting corruption: Whistleblowers

If a team member, attendee or volunteer observe or suspect corruption, can that person easily report it to the management of the event? Will they be rewarded or penalised? Is it discrete? The eyes and ears of the event are the staff. The aim of the perpetrator is to be undetected by the system. If a system is predictable, it can be bypassed, gamed and hacked. The team, attendees and volunteers, on the other hand, represent variety and unpredictability, i.e. uncertainty. It raises the cost of a corrupt act. The fact that reporting a corrupt act is easy to do and expected by the management is another preventive measure.

The expression *"blowing the whistle"* means providing information about alleged corrupt conduct. A whistleblower is a person who exposes the corruption within an organisation. Their motives can range from wanting the best for their organisation and fellow workers and nipping problems at the start, to simple revenge.

The International Standard, ISO 37002:2021, Whistleblowing Management Systems goes further to recommend a whistleblower system integrated into the overall management. The intended outcomes of having a complete whistleblower system are:

- It encourages reporting of wrongdoing.
- It supports and protects potential whistleblowers.
- It makes sure the wrongdoing is dealt with quickly and does not infect other parts of management.
- It acts as a preventative measure.
- It improves the organisational culture and governance.

(ISO, 37002:2021)

As to whether the event team can implement such a comprehensive system, considering the time and deadline issues, will be up to the risk management conclusions. However, it is worth noting there is a standard and, if the situation of the event is at this level, it can be called upon and enacted.

Having a whistleblower clause in the code of conduct may also prevent corruption as it increases the uncertainty of whether, in the future, the corrupt act will be found out. The perpetrator can never be sure if they will be exposed. This may reduce petty corruption as the cost is greater than the benefit. Although whistleblowing protection historically concerns government organisations and those who deal with it, it has now been expanded to corporations. The laws vary widely around the world. For example the EU Whistleblower Protection Directive (2019), although it includes private companies, the company must have more than 50 employees.

The recommendations of the various sporting codes and the UN on reporting corruption include:

1. Public interest disclosure of corruption should be encouraged.
2. The reporting of acts or suspicions should have confidential and easily available lines of communication such as private email, phone line. The complaint or allegation can be anonymous.
3. Ensure there is protection for the whistleblower and they do not suffer any negative consequences.
4. Check the relevant legislation.

Story 31: Interview with Di Henry: Systems, communication and morale

I spoke to Di Henry, about how she was able to traverse the world and organise multiple events of high complexity. This included being the Programme Director of Events at London 2012 Celebrations and Torch Relays of the Sydney Olympics, Asian Games and many other events in over 160 countries.

"For the Sydney Olympic and Paralympic Torch Relay, I had a day job the first year of creating and producing all of the Games announcements, launches, a six month series of parades celebration, capital city dinners for a thousand people and a travelling exhibition. Plus I managed to fit in 14 launches, announcements and more."

Setting up the governance of the Torch Relay was instrumental in her and her team's success in other mega events around the world.

"But my night job was to write all the policies and manuals that clearly laid out how the team and I would prepare and run the event. Operations Manuals, Risk Manuals, Media, Marketing and Sponsorship manuals, Torch Bearer selection systems, International Oceanic operations manuals, contracts, torch design competition, Day books and more."

As well as this aspect of governance, Di made sure that everyone was included.

"But behind all of my modus operandi was to include everyone and communicate with everyone. We wrote letters to all premiers and heads of territories asking them to form a committee with their representatives as chair, and to include representatives from Police, Ambulance, Tourism, Indigenous and Multicultural committees and who else they thought could contribute. I presented at those meetings with the advance managers for that state. We spoke about how many days we would be in their state, a proposed route and what support we needed."

Di stressed the importance of team morale and the informal elements needed.

"The core team in the office before you go on the road is about 20 people. In the build up I would take the team away for a weekend once a year. Loads of fun – bowling, being by the beach etc. Then once on the road, we had weekly dinners with a crew behind the scenes video and sometimes talent nights. To keep a team happy, they also like order and communications. Weekly work in progress meetings, creative and solutions meetings, and not all work, but some play after all"

Exercise

1. Research the code of conduct for festivals and conferences. How many of these have anti-corruption statements?
2. Using a sample event, develop a Code of Conduct for the event.
3. Di Henry's story is about engendering integrity through the intangible elements of good management. Discuss how you can prevent corruption by raising the morale of all who work for you.

Summary

- ☐ Governing Body
- ☐ Legal Environment, International, Regional, National, State, City, local Region, Association and Standards
- ☐ Event Policy
- ☐ Template of Policy
- ☐ Integrity
- ☐ Code of Conduct
- ☐ Whistleblowing

References

Graycar, A. (2015). Corruption: Classification and analysis, *Policy and Society* **34** (2015) 87–96

IS0. (2016). *Anti-bribery management systems — Requirements with guidance for use,* ISO 37001:2016. Switzerland: International Organization for Standardization

ISO (2021) *Whistleblowing Management Systems, ISO* 37002:2021. Switzerland: International Organization for Standardization.

Ivanov, E. (2022). *Overview of Anti-Corruption Compliance Standards and Guidelines.* 2ed. International Anti-Corruption Academy. Austria. www.iaca.int

Maesschalck, J. (2008). *Towards a Sound Integrity Framework: Instruments, Processes, Structures, and Conditions for Implementation.* Organisation de Coopération et de Développement Économiques. GOV/PGC(2008)21. Conference Paper in SSRN Electronic Journal

O'Toole, W.J. (2021). *Events Feasibility and Development: from Strategy to Operations.* 2nd Edition, UK: Routledge

Roth, L. (2013). *Corruption offences.* NSW Parliamentary Research Service. https://www.parliament.nsw.gov.au/researchpapers/Documents/corruption-offences/corruption%20offences.pdf

UN. (2013). *The United Nations Convention against Corruption: A Strategy for Safeguarding against Corruption in Major Public Events.* Vienna: United Nations Office on Drugs and Crime.

UN Global Compact Working Group. (2014). *Fighting Corruption in Sport Sponsorship and Hospitality: A practical guide for companies.* New York:United Nations. https://unglobalcompact.org/library/771

United States-Mexico-Canada Agreement (USMCA), Chapter 27: Anticorruption. https://ustr.gov/sites/default/files/files/agreements/FTA/USMCA/Text/27_Anticorruption.pdf

11 Vulnerability Assessment (exposure to corruption)

This chapter is a series of points the event team can consider to uncover any areas of their event and management vulnerable to the risk of corruption. It is based on the work of the UN, EU and others and adapted to an event project team. The output from the table should assist the creation of an Anti-Corruption Policy for the event. This is about risk minimisation. The table is not exhaustive. It is derived from the many UN documents and related documents and websites (see references), as well as the experience of the author and colleagues around the world in the events industry. It can be used as a checklist, aide-mémoire or assessment table.

It is a start and, as the corrupt are forever resourceful, it must be adapted and expanded for the specific cultural environment and the event. For a highly detailed questionnaire the reader should access the freely available UN 2013 *The United Nations Convention against Corruption: A Strategy for Safeguarding against Corruption in Major Public Events.* Download it from here:

www.unodc.org/documents/corruption/Publications/2013/13-84527_Ebook.pdf

Another tool used in creating the vulnerability assessment is the five dimensions of corruption based on the application of Professor Graycar's work and adding the dimension of time (Table 11.1: Five dimensions of corruption).

The planning of an event, it goes without saying and yet is too often forgotten, goes over a period of time. Every aspect has the time/cost/quality decision hanging over it. Identifying the most exposed times over the period is a way to prevent corruption. For example at a certain time the event team will have to decide on the suppliers. This is the time when bribery, such as kickbacks, favouritism and even extortion can take place.

Bringing in equipment and people from another country through the complexity of customs and immigration is another time to be aware of bribery demands or facilitation payments.

As illustrated by Story 27: *Gangsta Extortion* (p. 148), the most vulnerable time for an event is on the day and just before it starts. All the value, i.e. money, is riding on the smooth beginning of the event. The hustlers know this very well and it is surprising how they will use it to their advantage.

The event organisation can rate their vulnerability in the areas described using a scale of 0 to 10. The lower the mark the more vulnerable the event is to illegitimate activity. At the same time the rating indicates to the event team, the sponsors and the hosts, such as the local government, the level of good governance of the event. Shown in the table are the relevant chapters.

Once again we stress that corruption is secret. The table can only be an approximation based on experience. We welcome any reader input to strengthen this table. It will assist the whole event sector, push the Geryon away and ensure that trust is protected and integrity is paramount.

How to use the table

Follow the flowchart in Figure11.1.

1. Rate each row: 0 means it is not done at all; 5 means it is done but needs review; 10 means it is done to the best of our ability, is reasonably practicable and according to the law.
2. If the row does not concern your event, leave it blank.

3 Add up the scores and divide by the number of rows answered.

4 Multiply the figure by 10 to get a percentage rating.

5 Examine the row scores less than the 10 and decide on what actions need to be taken. These can be entered into the project plan for the event and the risk register, if necessary.

6 Once the event has concluded, re-examine the table to find what can be improved. This includes the table itself.

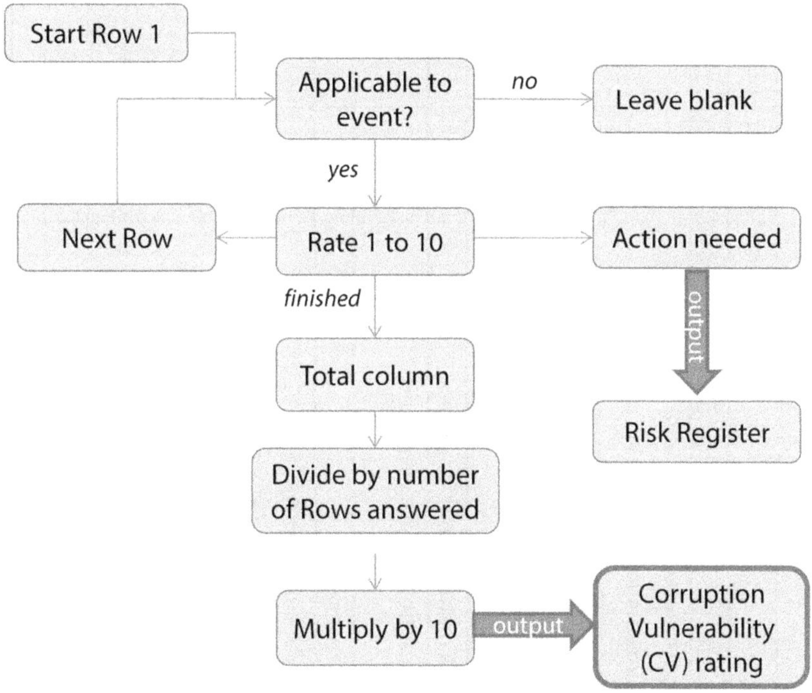

Figure 11.1: Flowchart to fill out Vulnerability table.

Table 11.1: Vulnerability table

Risk Area	Rating	Chapter	Action to take
Governance			
The event team is aware of the legal framework surrounding corruption, specifically how the sponsors' anti-corruption policies may impact the event both immediately and in the long term.		10	
Risk management embedded and the risk register is understood and used by the team.		7	
All team members are trained in risk management for events.		7, 9	
Project times of vulnerability to corruption are discussed and confirmed.		10	
Risk of corruption is part of the risk register.		7	
Leadership of the team is aware of the importance of setting the example of integrity for the team and temporary workers.		10	
The event board has undergone conflict of interest scrutiny		10	
The relationship between the Politically Exposed Persons (PEP), the board and the event team is clearly understood.		2	
Marketing			
The promotion or marketing person, department or company are creative without false hype.		5, 7	

Risk Area	Rating	Chapter	Action to take
They are aware of the immediate, mid and long term implications for the whole event, the team and their career of false information, exaggerated hype and fraud.		5, 7	
The marketing performance is evaluated using accurate data and realistic forecasts.		5, 7	
Outgoing and received gifts and hospitality are controlled via the gift register.		4, 7	
Last minute or emergency promotions must pass the designated authority before being released.		5, 7	
The final marketing report will include any instances of breach of code of conduct with regard to corruption.		10	
Finance			
Ensuring accurate estimation for the event budget prior to the event.		10	
A robust and trustworthy approval process for last minute payments.		10	
Accountable/recorded decisions for last minute and sudden increase in cost or funds.		4,5,7	
A process to check the over estimating or underestimating of costs.		4,5	

Risk Area	Rating	Chapter	Action to take
Aware of the key project times for vulnerability in finance: finding suppliers, contract negotiation, change requests, payment of invoices.		4,5 7, 10	
During the event: on-site payments and collection of cash by trained staff.		4	
Cross checking vendor payments to the event.		7	
Ensure all financial matters are recorded.		7,10	
Sponsorship			
The event organisation has a clear process and criteria to decide on sponsors, sponsorship type and levels.		10	
The event has a policy known to all the staff and volunteers on the acceptance of gifts or hospitality from the sponsors.		4, 7	
Any changes and developments of the sponsorship agreements are clearly authorised, recorded and report in a timely manner.		10	
The event team is aware of any anti-corruption policies of the sponsors of the event and how they apply to the event.		10	
Staff and Volunteers			
Recruitment is made on the basis of merit and competence.		8	
The criteria for employment and engagement clear and transparent to all.		8	

Risk Area	Rating	Chapter	Action to take
There is a straightforward and easy to understand code of conduct.		10	
All staff understands 'conflict of interest' and the process to disclose it.		6	
All staff understands nepotism/favouritism and the code of conduct and/or policy on this issue.		6	
Informal channels are open for the team to report any petty corruption.		8, 10	
They are aware of the formal and informal method of reporting instances of corruption.		8, 10	
There is special screening and monitoring for staff and volunteers in vulnerable positions such as payments of cash and managing overseas tours.		8	
Staff and volunteers are made aware of the ultimate effect of small 'grease' payments and given a script to avoid and decline them.		4, 8	
Security and reference checks are carried out for key employees.		8	
There is an easy to find and use gift or hospitality register.		4	
The four eyes principle is used if necessary.		8	

Risk Area	Rating	Chapter	Action to take
Procurement, contractors, vendors			
Procurement is achieved with clear evaluation criteria.		5	
Any possible conflicts of interest are known to the team and the risk is discussed.		6	
If the event involves government departments, the event procurement is in line with the government policy.		10	
Contractors/suppliers know the contract is invalid if there is proof of corruption.		5	
A clear "no bribery or kickbacks" statement or script that can be used by the team if offered a bribe.		10	
Contractor/supplier association has a clear anti-corruption policy and/or code of conduct.		10	
A clear, efficient process to decide on any amendments or other changes to the contract.		10	
A robust method to detect any false invoicing.		5	
An up-to-date database of alternative contractors and suppliers in case of default or corrupt practices.		5	
Vendors have a clear contract concerning any payments to the event including percentage of sales.		5	

Risk Area	Rating	Chapter	Action to take
Vendors are made aware of anti-corruption policy of the event and the penalties emphasising kickbacks, under reporting and gifts to staff.		5	
Ticketing			
Ticketing management policies or guidelines including appropriate processes and controls.		5	
Consideration of the vulnerable points for the events online presence: ticketing, online registration, mobile apps and wifi networks.		5	
On-site			
The permission areas, such as entrances, vendor placement, parking, back stage security, bar area, are understood to be prime areas for bribery and suitable precautions are taken.		4	
The four eyes principle considered for high risk areas and times on-site.		8	
Times during the event that can cover corrupt activity are identified.			
Blagging and other types of entrance fraud are understood and precautions taken.		5	

Risk Area	Rating	Chapter	Action to take
Estimates of crowds, before, during and after the event, are done as accurately as possible and not falsified purposely.		5	
On-site staff have a simple immediate reporting and recording system for any suspicious activity.		8	
Day volunteers understand the ongoing issues with petty corruption, such as extortion and legal penalties.		4	
Staff and volunteer rotation is used where suitable.		8.3	
The contractor's staff who deliver, set up, dismantle and return the on-site equipment understand there is an anti-corruption policy of the event.		5, 10	
The competition judges have been briefed on conflict of interest, favouritism, bribery and bias.		5	
Post event			
Archiving information for possible legal issues.		7	
Staff debrief includes the topics of corruption, such as gifts and facilitation payments.		4,5,6	

A Appendices

1: Anti-corruption policy template

This section has the main headings that have been extracted from a number of anti-corruption policy documents and applied to the events sector. As well there are suggestions for the information in the brackets [ ]. This is not complete. It is brief on purpose as there is always the temptation to "tick this box". Too much detail can be as dangerous as too little, because no one will read it or bother to understand it. Hence this must come from the risk management meetings where the team agree on its applicability to the specific event.

The information below must be adapted for the specific event and the legal socio/cultural environment.

1. Overview

[example "this policy sets out the standards and provides guidance on how to minimise corruption in the event planning, implementation and at the event venue or site"]

2. Message

[A personal message from the event team leader on the importance of integrity and the long term consequences of corrupt practices on the event, the event team and people's careers]

3. Scope

[Who does this policy apply to? Staff, volunteers, suppliers and any on-site personnel.]

4. Applicable laws

[e.g the UK Bribery Act 2010, the Commonwealth Criminal Code in Australia, the Canadian Corruption of Foreign Public Officials Act (CFPOA), the Foreign Corrupt Practices Act (FCPA) in the US.]

5. Key definitions

[Easy to understand definitions of the most likely types of corruption.]

6. Approach

- [The main sponsor or government department will have their own corruption control policy which can be referred to here.
- Corruption as a real risk that must prevented using a risk management approach.
- Describe prohibited conduct.
- On-site/ venue issues such as dealing with the public, gifts and facilitation payments
- Refer to the Code of Conduct, if it exists.
- Team must be aware that they and the event organisation may be liable for the corrupt practices of third parties associated with the event.]

7. Roles and Responsibilities

- [The person or team responsible for preventing, monitoring and managing the anti-corruption in the event project and the event site.
- The person to report to if corruption is suspected.
- The procurement team must ensure due diligence is performed on the suppliers prior to engagement.
- Event team must ensure the suppliers, vendors and volunteers are aware of the anti- corruption policy and if applicable, the code of conduct.]

8. Requirements of event team

- [All staff to attend and actively take part in the event risk management discussions and meetings.
- Event team staff should understand what corruption is, the types of corruption and the effects to the event and their careers.

- Each member must take seriously any reports of corruption from on-site staff, volunteers and attendees and report to relevant team member.
- The team must make sure suppliers, vendors and on-site staff are aware of the policies and the expectations with regard to any corruption.]

9. Breaches

[Depending on the severity of the corruption and its legal status the penalty can range from

- correction,
- warning,
- restricting to certain task or areas of responsibility,
- outright banning,
- legal charges.]

10. Extras

[Depending on the size of the event, the event budget and the level of corruption risk, there can be a section in the policy with examples and scenarios. Such as

" *A representative of the main sponsor of the event has asked you for ten extra tickets to the VIP area of the event. Although you have the authority to grant free tickets to the event, you need to ask the advice of the person on the event team who is responsible for anti-corruption and the request for extra tickets must be noted.* "]

2: AI and corruption

Machine learning needs large data to be effective. Large data needs stable parameters, variables and a classification (or category) system. The limitation is found in the word 'event'. It means out of the ordinary. The very basis of the event sector, the newness and innovation, is the issue when trying to construct a large data set. At the same time the basis of corruption is secrecy. It does not like to be recorded. So corruption can only be detected by proxies and anomalies. That is not to dismiss using Artificial Intelligence at all. Venues, for example, can use data collected over years to look for anomalies in supplier quotes. Although the events will come and go, the suppliers of many services such as sound, lights, food and beverage will be the same for many of the events. Also, as discussed in the section on fraud, the takings of the vendors at an event can be analysed. The parameters and variables include: size of crowd, demographics, position of the vendor on site, type of event and many more can create a matrix and used to identify anomalies in vendor reporting. Money laundering is a constant battle between the corrupt and the banks. The banks have sophisticated systems to filter data and the combination creates the red flags. But, then the corrupt ensure they are not caught by the filters. Every system can be gamed.

Any repeat event can collect longitudinal data and identify corruption. AI can easily predict what would be expected. This is why corruption in sports events is so quickly and easily recognised. As AI is more developed and the machine 'learns' more, we will see more and more sports exposed. The previously hidden, petty corruption will be uncovered as the machine learning exponentially increases. Exhibitions and conferences, as they are often a repeat event in standard venues can collect data. This can happen for the festivals, concerts and special events but its very newness works against the AI model. A local area with a centralised event team, such as a council area, already collects data about the events in their region. This is a valuable source for AI to trawl and look for patterns and anomalies. Figure A.1: *Anomaly detection using A.I* shows the schema where the AI uses pattern analysis to look for 'outliers' such as unusual transactions and proxy measures. This is currently performed with tools such as regression analysis and data analysis.

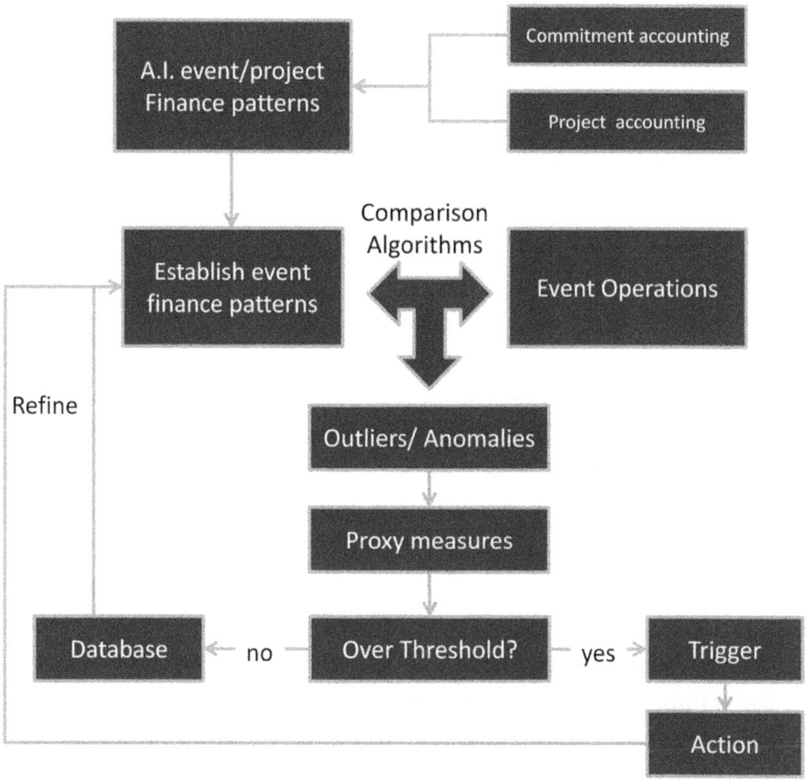

Figure A.1: Anomaly detection using A.I

However, as pointed out by the ICAC, the opportunities for corruption using AI are manifold. (OECD, 2024), (Legislative Council, 2024). The ability of AI to completely forge or subtly alter documents is a risk. It can include grant applications, guarantees to perform, databases, contracts, conflict of interest declarations, invoices, licenses and CVs. Photos, videos, music, emails, text messages or any other digital file can be changed. This can be difficult for a person to do, but is very easy using AI. A subtle change of a full stop in a quoted price can create chaos. The answer too often is that AI will pick up the fraud. But this is the snake biting its tail. If it can be picked up, it can be falsified.

Currently AI looks a threat to all digital communication and information. Verifying information must use a digital medium. That, in itself, can be easily falsified using AI. AI generated fraud and the like is only just starting. No guarantee anything that is delivered over a digital medium will be safe. This opens up a new Pandora's box.

Of interest the ICAC points out that these documents and other digital media can look genuine but be false because of the current limitations of AI. This eliminates any blame as there is no intention to deceive. (OECD, 2024)

References

Legislative Council. (2024). *Artificial intelligence in New South Wales, July 2024.* Portfolio Committee No. 1 - Premier and Finance. https://www.parliament.nsw.gov.au/lcdocs/inquiries/2968/Report%20No%2063%20-%20PC%201%20-%20Artificial%20intelligence%20in%20New%20South%20Wales%20-%2025%20July%202024.pdf

OECD. (2024). *Generative AI for Anti-Corruption and Integrity in Government.* OECD Artificial Intelligence Papers March 2024 No. 12. Paris: Public Governance Directorate. https://www.oecd.org/science/generative-ai-for-anti-corruption-and-integrity-in-government-657a185a-en.htm

3: Primary sources

Original documents and sites from around the world used in the distillation of anti-corruption theory and its application to events. These are in addition to those cited in the text and included in each chapter's references.

Alighieri, D. (2013). *The Divine Comedy* (C. James, Trans.). Picador.

Allens. (2021). *Anti-Bribery Policy*, Anti-Bribery Network. Document csjs 514060078v1 120972558. https://briberyprevention.com/

Attorney-General's Department. (2023). *Countering the Insider Threat.* Commonwealth Fraud Prevention Centre. https://www.ag.gov.au/sites/default/files/2023-05/countering-insider-threat-a-guide-for-australian-government-2023.PDF

Baker Mckenzie. (2017). *Global overview of Anti-Bribery Laws.* https://www.yumpu.com/en/document/read/58071958/global-overview-of-anti-bribery-laws-2017

Bayes Server. (2024). *Anomaly detection – an introduction.* https://www.bayesserver.com/docs/introduction/dynamic-bayesian-networks/

BDO. (2023). *AS 8001:2021 Fraud and Corruption Control - A Checklist for Boards and Executives.* https://www.bdo.com.au/en-au/home

Bouwens, J., Hofmann, C. & Lechner, C. (2022). *Transparency and Biases in Subjective Performance Evaluation*. TRR 266 Accounting for Transparency Working Paper Series No. 72. https://papers.ssrn.com/sol3/papers.cfm?abstract_id=4012905

Brandeis, L. (1914). *Other People's Money.* Chapter V: What Publicity Can Do. https://www.gutenberg.org/ebooks/57819

Cambodian Centre for Human Rights. (2011). *The Koh Pich Tragedy: One Year on, Questions Remain.* https://cchrcambodia.org/storage/posts/1538/2011-11-20-reports-eng-the-koh-pich-tragedy-one-year-on-questions-remain.pdf

China Daily. (2016). *Corruption, extravagance strictly checked around China's festivals.* https://www.chinadaily.com.cn/china/2016-09/15/content_26804544.htm

Coca-Cola Company. (2024). *Anti-Bribery Policy.* https://www.coca-colacompany.com/policies-and-practices/anti-bribery-policy

Department of Creative Industries, Tourism, Hospitality and Sport. (2024). *Fraud and Corruption Prevention Policy.* NSW Government. https://www.nsw.gov.au/departments-and-agencies/dciths/policies-plans-and-procedures/fraud-and-corruption-prevention-policy

Department of Homeland Security. (2018). *Outdoor Events Tabletop Exercise, Exercise Planner Handbook.* DHS.

DLA Piper. (2024). *Data Protection Laws of the World,* (https://www.dlapiperdataprotection.com/)

DOJ. (2019). *Two Boston City Hall Aides Convicted of Conspiring to Extort Music Festival Production Company.* https://www.justice.gov/usao-ma/pr/two-boston-city-hall-aides-convicted-conspiring-extort-music-festival-production-company

Federal Trade Commission Office of Inspector General, Whistleblower Protection, https://oig.ftc.gov/whistleblower-protection

Fielder, H. (2016). *Howard Marks: "We smuggled dope in the gear of bands like ELP, Floyd, Clapton".* Classic Rock. https://www.loudersound.com/features/howard-marks-we-smuggled-dope-in-the-gear-of-bands-like-elp-floyd-clapton

FIFA. (2020). *Compliance Handbook October 2020 edition.* https://inside.fifa.com/legal/compliance

Graycar, A. (2016). Corruption and Public Value. *Public Integrity,* 18(4), 339-341.

Graycar, A. and Jancsics, D. (2016). Gift Giving and Corruption. *International Journal of Public Administration.*

Graycar, A. and Masters, A. (2016). Making corruption disappear in local government. *Public Integrity,* **18**(1), 42-58.

Graycar, A. and Smith, R.G. (2011). *Global Handbook on Research and Practice in Corruption.* Cheltenham:Edward Elgar Publishing.

Hong Kong Business Ethics Development Centre. (2021). *Beware of the Laws when Presenting Gifts at Festivals.* https://hkbedc.icac.hk/

ICAC. (2000). *Practical Guide to Corruption Prevention*. Independent Commission Against Corruption. NSW Government. https://regulationbodyofknowledge.org/wp-content/uploads/2013/03/IndependentCommissionAgainstCorruption_Practical_Guide_to.pdf

ICAC. (2020). *Risk Management Policy No 81. Human Resources, Security & Facilities.* File Ref: :A20/0149 – D10696163. Independent Commission Against Corruption. NSW Government. https://www.icac.nsw.gov.au/ArticleDocuments/593/Policy%2081_risk%20management_August2020.pdf.aspx

ICAC. (2021a). *Advice on developing a fraud and corruption control policy* Independent Commission Against Corruption. NSW Government. www.icac.nsw.gov.au.

ICAC. (2021b). *Sample fraud and corruption control policy*. Independent Commission Against Corruption. NSW Government. https://www.icac.nsw.gov.au/

ICAC. (2023). *Fact Finder: A Guide To Conducting Internal Investigation*. Independent Commission Against Corruption. NSW Government. www.icac.nsw.gov.au.

International Chamber of Commerce (ICC). (2023). *ICC Rules on Combating Corruption* 2023 edition. https://2go.iccwbo.org/icc-rules-on-combating-corruption-2023.html.

International Partnership Against Corruption in Sport, Task Force 4. (2022). *Tackling bribery in sports: An overview of relevant laws and standards*. https://www.ipacs.sport/sites/default/files/2022-10/IPACS_Tackling_Bribery_in_Sport_An_Overview_of_Relevant_Laws_and_Standards.pdf

ISO, *IEC 31010:2019 - Risk Management - Risk Assessment Techniques*. Switzerland: International Organization for Standardization.

ISO, *ISO 31000:2018 - Risk Management - Principles and Guidelines*. Switzerland: International Organization for Standardization.

Jenkins, M. (2015). *Conflict of Interest: Topic Guide*. Transparency International. https://knowledgehub.transparency.org/assets/uploads/kproducts/Topic_Guide_Conflicts_of_Interest.pdf

Jones Day. (2018). *Anti-Corruption Regulation Survey of 41 Countries 2017-2018*. https://www.jonesday.com/en

Kerkhoff, T. (2018). *From moral-philosophical fiction to real political scenario's: why a particularistic focus on integrity should replace universal views on (anti) corruption.* https://blogs.sussex.ac.uk/centre-for-the-study-of-corruption/2018/11/14/the-current-failure-of-anti-corruption/

Köbis, N. Starke, C. & Rahwan, I. (2021). *Artificial Intelligence as an Anti-Corruption Tool - A Conceptual Framework.* https://arxiv.org/abs/2102.11567

Leeson, P. (2009). *The Invisible Hook: The Hidden Economics of Pirates.* Oxford:Princeton University Press.

Levitt, S. D. & Dubner, S. J. (2005). *Freakonomics: A rogue economist explores the hidden side of everything*. William Morrow & Co.

Lion. (2022). *Anti-Bribery and Corruption Policy,* December 2022. https://lionenergy.com.au/wp-content/uploads/2023/04/LIO-POL-011_Anti-Bribery-and-Corruption-Policy-2022.pdf

New South Wales Consolidated Acts. *CRIMES ACT 1900 - SECT 249B Corrupt commissions or rewards.* https://www5.austlii.edu.au/au/legis/nsw/consol_act/ca190082/s249b.html

New Zealand Events Association (NZEAP). (2020). *Principles of Professional and Ethical Conduct.* https://www.nzea.co/

OECD-IPACS. (2019). *Mitigating Corruption Risks in the Procurement of Sporting Events.* (OECD) International Partnership Against Corruption in Sport (IPACS), https://www.ipacs.sport/sites/default/files/2019-12/mitigating-corruption-risks-procurement-sporting-events-IPACS.pdf

Pohekar, P. (2014). Corruption prevention measures recommended by Kautilya. *Socrates,* **2**(2).

Santos, G., Gursoy, D., Ribeiro, M. & Netto, A. (2019). Impact of transparency and corruption on mega-event support. *Event Management,* **23**, 27–40

SEC. (2015). *SEC Charges BHP Billiton With Violating FCPA at Olympic Games.* https://www.sec.gov/news/press-release/2015-93

SEC. (2023). *Administrative Proceeding File* No. 3-21581 www.sec.gov/files/litigation/admin/2023/34-98222.pdf

Teck. (2020). *Anti-Corruption Compliance Policy & Manual.* Canada. https://www.teck.com/

The Association of Insurance and Risk Managers in Industry and Commerce (AIRMIC). (2023). *Scenario Analysis A Practical Guide Helping to develop insight and manage uncertainty.* www.airmic.com

The State Library of NSW. (2022). *Fraud and Corruption Prevention Policy.* https://www.sl.nsw.gov.au/sites/default/files/slnsw_fraud_corruption_prevention_policy.pdf

Transparency International (TI). (2022a). *Corruptionary A-Z.* https://www.transparency.org/en/corruptionary

United Nations Office on Drugs and Crime (UNODC). (2013). *Safeguarding against Corruption in Major Public Events: Participant Manual,* https://www.unodc.org/documents/corruption/Publications/Major_Public_Events_Training_Materials/Facilitators_Guide_Safeguarding_against_Corruption_in_MPE.pdf

United Nations Office on Drugs and Crime(UNODC). (2017). *Handbook on Anti-Corruption Measures in Prisons.* https://www.unodc.org/documents/justice-and-prison-reform/17-06140_HB_anti-corr_prisons_eBook.pdf

UNODC. (n/d). *Tools and Resources for Anti-Corruption Knowledge (TRACK).* (https://track.unodc.org/)

Willems, A., Tagliaferri, M., & Theodorakis, N. (2016). *Corruption risk assessment tools in customs and trade.* OECD Integrity Forum, Paris. https://www.tralac.org/images/docs/9497/corruption-risk-assessment-tools-in-customs-and-trade-2016-oecd-integrity-forum-paper.pdf

Wrage, A. A. (2007). *Bribery and Extortion: Undermining Business, Governments, and Security.* Westport,: Praeger Security International

Wu, W. & Fong K. (2022). Perceived impact on holding serial mega events: do perceived government corruption matter? A case study on Macao young residents. *Conference Proceedings 2021.* Cape Town: Cape Peninsular University of Technology.

4: Acronyms

ACCC Australian Competition and Consumer Commission

ALARP As Low As Reasonably Practicable

BPFI Banking and Payments Federation Ireland

CBA Cost/benefit analysis

CCDI Central Commission for Discipline Inspection

CiC Commercial in Confidence

CISA U.S. Cybersecurity and Infrastructure Security Agency

CTR currency transaction reporting

DOJ US Department of Justice

FATF Financial Action Task Force

ICAC Independent Commission Against Corruption

ICC International Chamber of Commerce

ICGN International Corporate Governance Network

IPACS International Partnership Against Corruption in Sport

ISO International Organization for Standardization

LOPA Layers of Protection Analysis

NDA Non Disclosure Agreement

PEP Politically Exposed Persons

SEC Securities and Exchange Commission

TI Transparency International

UEFA Union of European Football Associations

UN United Nations

UNODC United Nations Office on Drugs and Crime

Index

www.ingramcontent.com/pod-product-compliance
Ingram Content Group UK Ltd.
Pitfield, Milton Keynes, MK11 3LW, UK
UKHW020657151224
452011UK00007B/31

9 781915 097996